Brain Changers

Brain Smart

The Brain Smart series consists of three books, offering readers a wide range of tools and information to support your child's learning brain. Using up-to-date research and hands-on learning strategies, parents can explore how children learn at all grade levels and ages. Book one, *A Guide to How Your Child Learns: Understanding the Brain from Infancy to Young Adulthood* features 60 relevant and digestible articles about your child's learning brain. Book two, *Brain Changers: Major Advances in Children's Learning and Intelligence* explores notable learning theorists who have defined major advancements in learning at the highest levels in education, child development, and neuropsychology.

My third book, *Brain Gains: So, You Want to be Your Child's Learning Coach?* (2020) concludes the Brain Smart Trilogy with hands-on learning techniques and easy-to-implement strategies to support crucial information from my first two books.

In closing, the Brain Smart trilogy integrates major areas of learning, child development, and psychology with up-to-date research.

David P. Sortino Ed.M, Ph.D.
Graton, CA, 2019

Brain Changers

*Major Advances in
Children's Learning and Intelligence*

David P. Sortino

ROWMAN & LITTLEFIELD
Lanham • Boulder • New York • London

Published by Rowman & Littlefield
An imprint of The Rowman & Littlefield Publishing Group, Inc.
4501 Forbes Boulevard, Suite 200, Lanham, Maryland 20706
www.rowman.com

6 Tinworth Street, London SE11 5AL

Copyright © 2020 by David P. Sortino

All rights reserved. No part of this book may be reproduced in any form or by any electronic or mechanical means, including information storage and retrieval systems, without written permission from the publisher, except by a reviewer who may quote passages in a review.

British Library Cataloguing in Publication Information Available

Library of Congress Cataloging-in-Publication Data

Library of Congress Control Number: 2019951024
ISBN 978-1-4758-3179-5 (cloth : alk paper)
ISBN 978-1-4758-3180-1 (pbk : alk paper)
ISBN 978-1-4758-3181-8 (electronic)

∞ ™ The paper used in this publication meets the minimum requirements of American National Standard for Information Sciences Permanence of Paper for Printed Library Materials, ANSI/NISO Z39.48-1992.

Contents

Brain Changing Quotes — vii

Author's Note — ix

Acknowledgments — xi

Introduction — xiii

1 Cognition: Understanding How Children Learn and Express Their Intelligence—Dr. Jean Piaget (1900–1981) — 1

2 Multiple Intelligence: Identifying Your Child's True Intelligence —Dr. Howard Gardner (1943–) — 23

3 Psychosocial Development: Tapping into Your Child's Social Intelligence —Dr. Erik Erikson (1902–1994) — 53

4 Moral Development: The Development of the Moral Child — Dr. Lawrence Kohlberg (1927–1987) — 63

5 Vocational Intelligence: It Is Never Too Early to Attach a Child's Passion to Their True Intelligence—John Holland (1919–2008) — 79

6 Thinking: Raising Children's Thinking Skills Increases Intelligence and Learning—Edward de Bono (1933–) — 99

7 Neurofeedback: How Brain Training Can Increase Your Child's Learning and Intelligence — 107

Appendix — 121

Bibliography	125
Index	139
About the Author	145

Brain Changing Quotes

Chapter 1: Cognition: Understanding How Children Learn and Express their Intelligence

"Educators are not neuroscientists, but they are members of the only profession in which their job is to change the human brain every day"—Dr. David A. Sousa

Chapter 2: Multiple Intelligence: Identifying Your Child's True Intelligence

"I saw the angel in the marble and carved until I set him free"—Michelangelo

Chapter 3: Psychosocial Development: Tapping into Your Child's Social Intelligence

"You see a child play, and it is so close to seeing an artist paint, for in play a child says things without uttering a word. You can see how he solves his problems. You can also see what's wrong. Young children, especially, have enormous creativity, and whatever's in them rises to the surface in free play."—Dr. Erik Erikson

Chapter 4: Moral Development: The Development of the Moral Child

"Because power corrupts, society's demands for moral authority and character increase as the importance of the position increases."—John Adams

Chapter 5: Vocational Intelligence: It Is Never Too Early to Attach a Child's Passion to Their True Intelligence

"But when you're in front of an audience and you make them laugh at a new idea, you're guiding the whole being for the moment. No one is ever more him/herself than when they really laugh. Their defenses are down. It's very Zen-like, that moment. They are completely open, completely themselves when that message hits the brain and the laugh begins. That's when new ideas can be implanted. If a new idea slips in at that moment, it has a chance to grow."—George Carlin

Chapter 6: Thinking: Raising Children's Thinking Skills Increases Intelligence and Learning

"Thinking is like walking or breathing. There is nothing we need to do about it. There is nothing we can do about it. Any interference with it will only make it awkward and artificial and inhibited by self-consciousness. If you are intelligent you are a good thinker. If you are not intelligent that's too bad and you should listen to someone who is."—Dr. Edward de Bono

Chapter 7: Neurofeedback: How Brain Training Can Increase Your Child's Learning and Intelligence

"The literature, which lacks any negative study of substance, suggests that EEG biofeedback [neurofeedback] therapy should play a major therapeutic role in many difficult areas. In my opinion, if any medication had demonstrated such a wide spectrum of efficacy, it would be universally accepted and widely used."—Dr. Frank Duffy, neurologist, Harvard Medical School

Author's Note

It all began when my parents placed a net over my crib or brain!

Malcolm Gladwell's book *Outliers* describes the 10,000-hour journey, or how it takes 10,000 hours of focus and hard work to achieve a Bill Gates type of expertise and/or success. I do not pretend that I am remotely like Bill Gates, but my life's work as a learning specialist, aka "brain changer," has felt like a 10,000-hour journey. Any success I have had is attributable to personal learning experiences, coupled with the learning techniques I describe in this book as "brain changing."

My 10,000-hour journey as a learning specialist began as an eighteen-month-old toddler when I deliberately and repeatedly attempted to escape my crib (at all hours of the night). Years later, I realized this was merely a developmental stage. My innocent crib experiences were later defined by developmental psychologist Dr. Erik Erickson as a stage called "autonomy versus doubt and shame." In many respects, it was this connection to my own behavior that began my journey as a learning specialist.

In my view, the positive learning experiences of my nightly attempts to escape the crib were about learning to be autonomous from parental controls and not to feel the slightest *shame or doubt*, until I was grounded when my parents placed a net over my crib, and my brain. Still, such creative learning experiences have stayed with me to this day.

At age eight, a traumatic third-grade experience coincided with what Erikson defined as the "industry versus inferiority" stage. In fact, I am sure that my need at the time to make the negative (inferiority) rather than the positive (industry) choice was directly connected to my refusal to accept the academic status quo of any learning paradigm, which required me to sit in a seat for lengthy periods of the day! My acting-out behavior elicited a trip to see a psychiatrist, who pronounced me only a normal boy, and perhaps my teacher would take him up on a free therapy session?

Such behavior followed me through most of grade school, middle school, and high school. There were more refusals to accept the status quo. I deliberately failed a placement exam at a private Catholic high school, which resulted in a designated learning status in a class called "zoo zoo," an event that could be translated into Erikson's adolescent stage of "identity versus role confusion."

However, I had no confusion about my classmates' learning identities, which according to some of our teachers were almost nonexistent and due in part to our teachers' refusal to see the true genius of these "zoo zoo" students.

In other words, it was this "zoo zoo" grouping that gave me added insight into Dr. Howard Gardner's theory of multiple intelligence, a valuable concept discussed in this book's chapter 2 and a notable brain changer. Interestingly, whenever a teacher needed their car tuned up or an artist to paint the backdrop for our school plays, they always turned to the "zoo zoo" crowd, because their genius was more in line with kinesthetic and artistic intelligence—thank you, Dr. Gardner!

Years later, as a teacher at a day treatment school for seriously emotionally disturbed and learning handicapped children, I was able to take my so-called negative school learning experiences and apply them successfully to children with serious learning and behavior disorders. This experience provided me with the impetus to write a book called *The Promised Cookie: No Longer Angry Children* (2011). It was at this school that I first employed successful brain changing techniques with such difficult learners.

In addition, recently I published my first book in the Brain Smart series, *A Guide to How Children Learn: Understanding Learning from Infancy to Early Adulthood* (2017), which serves as a precursor to this book.

Author and renowned learning specialist Dr. David Sousa said it best when he explained that "educators are not neuroscientists, but they are members of the only profession in which their job is to change the human brain every day." In my opinion, what Dr. Sousa was really saying is that if you truly want to become a successful brain changer, you need to recognize that learning is developmental or constantly changing, and the more we support this fact, the greater our success will be in using the brain changing concept with children of all ages.

Dr. David P. Sortino, 2019

Acknowledgments

I wish to acknowledge all those individuals who contributed to the creation of this book. My family: Jennifer, Abby, and Shai; my students, clients, and editors: Ms. Jan Corbett, Ms. Carol Vacek, and Ms. Laurie Hagar Bush; and of course Henry, our pug!

Moreover, *brain changing* is synonymous with *brain changers*, which is why I must acknowledge those professionals who are listed in this book as brain changers: Daniel Amen, B. S. Bloom, G. Carlin, Edward de Bono, Howard Gardner, W. Huitt, Lawrence Kohlberg, Thomas Lickona, Margaret Mahler, Mandy Manning, Michelangelo, Maria Montessori, Joseph Chilton Pearce.

Introduction

Brain Changers: Major Advances in Children's Learning and Intelligence is the second book of the Brain Smart series. The first book, *A Guide to How Your Child Learns: Understanding the Brain from Infancy to Early Adulthood*, presents information on how children learn at different stages of brain development. *Brain Changers*, however, gives an in-depth examination of *brain changing techniques* for children at all stages of brain development. In fact, the words *brain changing* reflect an often ignored concept: that *every learning experience requires brain change*, or what neuroscientists refer to as *brain plasticity*, which is the brain's ability to modify its connections or rewire itself. Studies show that without this ability, any brain, not just the human brain, would be unable to develop from infancy to adulthood (Banks, 2016).

For this reason, I dedicate this book to every individual who is or has been in a position to be a (so-called) *brain changer*. Teachers, parents, psychologists, learning specialists, school counselors—the list is endless. All participate in this challenge on a daily basis, yet in my view, recognition of their importance is limited. Again, borrowing a phrase from noted psychologist and learning specialist Dr. David Sousa: educators are not neuroscientists, but they are members of the only profession in which their job is to change the human brain every day.

The phrase *brain changing* supports the *obvious* concept that when learners are interested or passionate about the learning process, they usually learn best. In fact, our brain's limbic system understands this when it forms emotional connections or attachments (bonding) to an important part of our brain called the hippocampus. According to some neuroscientists, the reason the brain's hippocampus is so important to brain changing is because the hippocampus is considered the only part of the learning brain where neurons regenerate or make new neurons.

In my many years as a learning specialist, almost every successful student's or client's learning experience was the result of the learner having had an *emotional* brain changing experience. For instance, an examination of how children learn to read could tell us how the physiology of the brain reacts during a positive or negative brain changing experience.

Specifically, if one area of the child's brain exhibits problems recognizing letters and knowing which sounds the letters make, they may have a learning condition called dyslexia. As a result, the child could then view learning to read as a negative experience, and the child's thalamus, located in the brain's limbic system, could interpret the experience as negative and send an impulse to the amygdala, which releases the chemical cortisol, causing a fight-or-flight response. In short, this response could short-circuit the left linguistic area of the child's brain, which is responsible for reading, language development, and the like.

However, if the reading experience is *positive* , the hippocampus, located on the left side of the brain, bonds with the experience and connects with the brain's executive areas, and a potential positive reading experience can occur. Again, the medical world understands this positive learning experience and describes the function as brain plasticity, or the brain's ability to modify its connections or rewire itself.

The recognition of brain changers not only acknowledges individuals such as teachers, parents, and counselors but also points to the innovative techniques used by them to support this difficult task, what I, again, call *brain changing*.

For example, brain changing techniques have been around for years. Dr. Maria Montessori, a noted brain changer, used specific brain changing techniques with orphaned children by connecting the child's lack of maternal touch and bonding to the child's ability to learn how to read. With the help of "sandpaper letters," Montessori's children could simultaneously say or sing the alphabet or phonemes while touching the letters.

In other words, Montessori smartly connected the need for touch (kinesthetic intelligence) in orphaned children with their ability to bond (hippocampus) with letters, words, and reading in general.

Rudolf Steiner of Waldorf Education developed a brain changing curriculum that integrated the arts with education, including dance, music, drama, calligraphy, and more, within a general school curriculum. Both educational philosophies are excellent examples of the brain changing concept, or neuroplasticity, which I will present in this book.

Moreover, Swiss developmental psychologist Dr. Jean Piaget studied and established brain changing theories on how children process information at every age and stage of life. Interestingly, much of Piaget's cognitive development theories laid the foundation for school curriculums and learning paradigms currently in use throughout the world.

Brain changing research did not occur just in our schools. Neuroscientist Eleanor Maguire demonstrated larger hippocampi in the brains of London cabdrivers. This was because London cabdrivers spent two to three years memorizing London's intricate street grids, including the shortest distance between two points. Using a magnetic resonance imagining (MRI) scanner, Maguire found that the cabbies' right posterior hippocampi, a region devoted to spatial navigation, measured 7 percent larger than the norm. Evidently, neuroplasticity had shaped the cabbies' brains as they learned more and more about navigating through London (Brown, 2009).

In addition, even the school schedule can produce brain changing effects with student learning. For instance, the first twenty minutes of each school day is a most impactful learning time, and an understanding of the importance of this open period is the reason why teachers *should not* waste this critical period of the school day on such mundane tasks as taking attendance or lunch count. Studies describe this impact as the *primacy–recency effect*, or the conundrum that the brain remembers best what comes *first* and *last* and retains less of what is in the *middle*.

Therefore, it makes sense for teachers to begin the school day by connecting the day's most important information to the previous day's lessons, a practice shown to activate higher learning for students. (This procedure is also referred to as the "anticipatory set.")

Additionally, the primacy–recency effect points to the last twenty minutes as a critical time as well. Teachers should consider organizing the school day's last twenty minutes accordingly. You can test out this concept by asking your students or child what they remembered from the previous school day.

Another important concept that adds critical information to the brain changing repertoire is Dr. Howard Gardner's *eight multiple intelligence types*. Specifically, when you can define a child's particular or preferred intelligence, you are in essence attaching an emotional component to the brain's hippocampus (bonding), which creates a road map to your child's executive learning centers. In addition, integrating multiple intelligence theory into a school curriculum creates an interdisciplinary approach and has been shown to be successful in many school programs, such as Montessori, Steiner, and other methods.

A major contributor to the brain changing concept is Erik Erikson's psychosocial theory. Erik Erikson (1902–1994) was a stage theorist who modified Freud's psychosexual theory to create eight stages of psychosocial development (trust vs. mistrust, autonomy vs. shame/doubt, initiative vs. guilt, industry vs. inferiority, identity vs. role confusion, intimacy vs. isolation, generativity vs. stagnation, and integrity vs. despair). (Google Freud's psychosexual theory for additional information.) Erikson's eight stages defines two opposing ideas that individuals need to resolve successfully to become a so-called positive contributor to society. In truth, an inability to accomplish this can lead to a lack of accomplishment in other areas of human development.

John Holland's theory of vocational development made a significant contribution to this book. Holland's theory supports psychology and vocational development with an easy-to-apply assessment by identifying six career types or themes, helpfully summarized as RIASEC (realistic, investigative, artistic, social, enterprising, and conventional).

Another crucial brain changing concept in this book is called *thinking*. That is, do we really provide children with opportunities to improve their thinking abilities or skills? We teach children about learning, rules and consequences in the home and school, but do we really address how children can improve their ability to think?

Borrowing insightful thinking techniques from distinguish scholar Dr. Edward de Bono's famous book *The Thinking Course*, we delve into various techniques to improve children's thinking abilities at all grade levels.

Moral development could be the most important concept in this book for the simple reason that moral judgment is seriously being challenged for today's youth from so many directions. Whether it is the proliferation of electronics and social media or the effects of peer groups, parents, teachers, and others who teach children are being put to the test and looking for real answers on how to cope with these challenges.

Introduction

Above all, I have included a chapter about moral development principally because of my many years conducting moral development groups with at-risk youth, and also because of my studies with Dr. Lawrence Kohlberg and associates at Harvard's Center for Moral Development. In short, these experiences helped solidify a greater understating of my relationships to students, clients, and others in need.

In closing, I believe the chapter on moral development could serve as the glue holding together this book's other chapters, covering topics such as cognitive development and multiple intelligence, offering well-rounded approaches to brain changing for children of all ages.

I conclude this book with a chapter on neurofeedback. This chapter describes how neurofeedback (brain changing) can successfully work together to stimulate higher learning potential with individuals at all levels. From the ADHD child's inability to focus and function in the classroom to the professional athlete who strives to find his or her competitive zone, neurofeedback can help individuals in all walks of life. (Note that the American Academy of Pediatrics has defined neurofeedback as the number one alternative to medication for ADHD children.)

This book represents my forty-plus years as a brain changer, describing the employment of many successful techniques and information listed in this book. Good luck, and please email me (davidsortino@comcast.net) about your use of the brain changing techniques shown in this book.

Chapter One

Cognition

Understanding How Children Learn and Express Their Intelligence—Dr. Jean Piaget (1900–1981)

Dr. Jean Piaget was a Swiss developmental psychologist and is a major contributor to the theory of cognitive development. Piaget defined five stages of cognitive development and provided valuable information to the field of developmental psychology and education about how children learn, think, and problem solve at different ages or stage. Piaget placed great importance on the education of children.

Barry Wadsworth's excellent book *Piaget's Theory of Cognitive and Affective Development* (1984) speaks to the heart of every parent's and teacher's dilemma—when to help or not help a child struggling with a learning experience—or as Wadsworth says, "preventing the child's brain from figuring it out." Wadsworth goes on to say, "Children are motivated to restructure their knowledge when they encounter experiences that conflict with their predictions." Piaget called this occurrence *disequilibration*, and the result of it *disequilibrium*. Some have called it *cognitive conflict*.

To the extent that educators are interested in helping children acquire knowledge, they must develop methods that encourage disequilibrium and permit children to carry out in their own ways the establishment of equilibrium through active methods of *assimilation and accommodation*. Wadsworth asks the million-dollar question: "How can disequilibrium be recognized and encouraged by the teacher?" (p. 17).

The key is to realize that disequilibrium should be recognized as a natural cognitive act. That is, unless parents or teachers realize this point, cognitive development could be stifled and lessened. The beauty of this chapter's information is that it speaks to this dilemma by attaching Piaget's cognitive stages to learning. Additionally, in this chapter teachers and parents will learn *when to help* and *when not to help* the child by understanding that the child's cognitive stage is directly linked to the hows, whens, and whys of learning.

A study by Huitt and Hummel (2003) describes the different cognitive stages that high school teachers face in a normal public school classroom. For example, the study found that the percentage of students thinking at Piaget's *formal operational stage*, generally considered our highest stage of cognitive development, were as follows: in ninth grade, 20 percent; in tenth, 25 percent; in eleventh, 30 percent; and in twelfth, 35 percent.

As you will read in the following pages, the importance of the different percentages illustrates why teachers and parents need to have a serious understanding of how cognition and our learning brain is connected. The connection begins with the school curriculum and carries over to the many nuances associated with the various stages of cognitive development.

Again, from ninth through twelfth grade, Huitt's study found that many high school student are still reasoning at the lower stage of *concrete operational thinking*—the level of most seven- to eleven-year-olds!

Furthermore, at age eleven, middle school should usher in the beginning of formal operational thinking. The inability for more middle school students to perform at beginning formal operational thinking (10 percent) may be why so few twelfth graders scored at formal operational thinking.

A second study by Huitt et al. (2003) addressed the effect multiple cognitive stages could have on classroom learning and school success. The existence of multiple cognitive stages, often in single classrooms and among students of the same age, comes in conflict with mandated school curriculums, testing, length of school year or length of school day, and much more. In other words, if the (multiple) classroom stages below are considered normal, *how does a teacher with twenty-plus children teach a class with multiple cognitive stage*s?

Here's a summary of Huitt's findings:

- Five-year-olds: 80 percent preoperational; 20 percent concrete operations (onset)

- Six-year-olds: 60 percent preoperational; 30 percent concrete operations (onset); 10 percent concrete operations (mature)
- Seven-year-olds: 30 percent preoperational; 60 percent concrete operations (onset); 10 percent concrete operations (mature)
- Eight-year-olds: 25 percent preoperational; 55 percent concrete operations (onset); 20 percent concrete operations (mature)
- Nine-year-olds: 15 percent preoperational; 50 percent concrete operations (onset); 35 percent concrete operations (mature)
- Ten-year-olds: 10 percent preoperational; 50 percent concrete operations (onset); 35 percent concrete operations (mature); 5 percent formal operations (onset)
- Eleven-year-olds: 10 percent preoperational; 40 percent concrete operations (onset); 30 percent concrete operations (mature); 10 percent formal operations (onset)
- Twelve-year-olds: 5 percent preoperational; 30 percent concrete operations (onset); 45 percent (mature); 20 percent formal operations (onset)
- Thirteen-year-olds: 4 percent preoperational; 25 percent concrete operations (onset); 40 percent concrete operations (mature); 20 percent formal operations (onset); 10 percent formal operations (mature)
- Fourteen-year-olds: 1 percent preoperational; 29 percent concrete operations (onset); 40 percent concrete operational (mature); 20 percent formal operations (onset); 10 percent formal operations (mature)

That is to say, some students are moving into one cognitive stage while other students are leaving. All the while, the teacher must teach within a mandated curriculum. Include divorce, separation, poor diet, and electronic distractions and one begins to see the problem teachers face on a daily basis.

Brain Changing Note: Again, to quote renown learning specialist Dr. David Sousa, "Educators are not neuroscientists, but they are members of the only profession in which their job is to change the human brain every day."

As you read and learn about different cognitive stages, you will be reminded why the teaching profession must be considered a most difficult job. The tragedy is how rarely this important problem of students' multiple cognitive stages is discussed by the powers that be. Therefore, teachers and parents might wish to read this chapter *more than once* so that they have a good understanding of the effect cognitive development can have on learning and student success.

PIAGET'S STAGES OF COGNITIVE DEVELOPMENT

Stage 0: Sensory and Motor, Ages 0–2

Our first stage is called the *sensory and motor stage*. In this crucial developmental period, the child's learning and intelligence are directed through his five senses and processed particularly in the brain's cerebellum or "old brain." The cerebellum controls the body's ability to maintain balance and coordination, but recently brain scientists have discovered that the cerebellum plays an important role in learning, particularly reading, writing, and math.

Brain Changing Note: Piaget theorized that even the youngest infants learn how to make sense of their environments. According to Piaget, "knowledge is organized into different schemas, or sets of mental representations about the environment. When a new object or situation is encountered, it will either be assimilated [digested] into an existing mental representation (if it is consistent with the schema), or it will be accommodated by changing an existing mental representation (if it is inconsistent with that schema). Intellectual development occurs through a continual process of assimilation of new information, and accommodation, that is updating existing schemas to reflect new knowledge" (Schonberg, 2013).

Brain Changing Note: "Three to four years between kids? This spacing generally produces less chaos in the home than a two-year gap because the older child is gaining self-sufficiency and may even be helpful when the baby arrives. Many of the same financial benefits of the two-year difference still apply here, like reduced costs for both kids in childcare, schools and college. Similarly, you already have most of the gear you'll need. The financial drawbacks aren't huge compared to the two-year gap—you may pay more for individual kid activities since your children won't share the same skill sets until late elementary school" (Forbes, 2012).

Brain Changing Note: Google Dr. David Sortino, "Why French Kids Do Not Have ADHD."

Further, we need to take heed of the effect *organization and predictability* plays when addressing your child's learning brain throughout each cognitive developmental stage. In my opinion, the first time the infant cries and demands to have his needs met is the brain's cry for *organization and predictability* from his caregivers. Parents who do not respond or who fail to meet the infant's needs with a predictable and organized response or schedule (feeding, changing diapers, etc.) could cause a lack of trust or bonding (reactive attachment disorder) that could directly affect the child's future learning experiences and even the development of intelligence.

Brain Changing Note: "Reactive attachment disorder is a rare but serious condition in which an infant or young child doesn't establish healthy attachments with parents or caregivers. Reactive attachment disorder may develop if the child's basic needs for comfort, affection and nurturing aren't met and loving, caring, stable attachments with others are not established" (Mayo Clinic, 2017). For more, Google Dr. David Sortino, "Teaching Students with Attachment Disorders."

Bottom line: future learning situations are being developed at this stage of infancy. The examples below provide a brief explanation of what your child is capable of achieving at various cognitive stages or ages, from infancy to toddlerhood, and suggest why *organization and predictability* are crucial to brain changing.

0–1 month: The infant's intelligence is based on *reflex*. Infants see no difference between themselves and other objects. They are purely *egocentric*, and much of their behavior is based on *instinct*. Therefore, their caregivers should be highly sensitive to the infant's needs. Briefly, parents and caregivers must help the infant develop a trusting intelligence since trust or bonding is a major precursor to future learning potential and the development of intelligence.

Brain Changing Note: Hungarian-born psychiatrist Margaret Mahler (1897–1985) worked first in her native Hungary and then in Britain and finally in the United States. She is best known for originating the *separation–individuation theory* of child development. In her theory, Mahler speculates that after the first few weeks of infancy, in which the infant is either sleeping or barely conscious, the infant progresses first from a phase (normal-symbiotic phase) in which it perceives itself as one with its mother within the larger environment, to an extended phase (separation-individuation phase) consisting of several stages or subphases in which the infant slowly comes to distinguish itself from its mother, and then, by degrees, discovers its own identity, will, and individuality (SCRIBD, 2018).

1–4 months: The infant is capable of coordinating mouth and hand through sucking or grasping. Any change in behavior is relative to the objects presented. Probably his first feelings of joy, happiness, and unpleasantness occur in this period.

4–8 months: The infant's eye–hand coordination will become evident immediately. They are actually interested in what the hand is doing. I learned this lesson about their new ability to anticipate positions of moving objects when I placed a mobile over my seven-month-old daughter's crib, which only lasted until she violently ripped it down to her delight! Further, infants at this age see themselves as the cause of all events, but generally have no (spatial) relationship to objects. In other words, they cannot anticipate what will happen when they start flinging their hands wildly over the Cheerios that are on the highchair tray. *Imagine that! The Cheerios end up on the kitchen floor!*

8–12 months: Infants can now coordinate and anticipate objects like a bottle or nipple. They now possess the skill called *object permanence* (tracking). They use higher intelligence to feed themselves and are actually learning to problem solve by coordinating hands with the mouth, particularly with food. They can turn the nipple or bottle right-side-up to get to the nipple.

Brain Changing Note: "When does the infant first come to view himself as a separate entity, an incipient person. It is possible, unbeknownst to the child to place a tiny marker—for example, a daub of rouge—upon his nose and then to study his reactions as he peers at himself in a mirror. During the first year of life, the infant is amused by the rouge marking but apparently simply regards it as an interesting decoration on some organism which he happens to be examining in the mirror. However, during the second year of life, the child will come to react differently when he beholds the alien coloring. Children will touch their own noses and act silly or coy when they encounter this unexpected redness on what they perceive to be their very own anatomy" (Gardner, 1983).

12–18 months: An infant can actually experiment and sequence missing objects. *Let's see—it was here and then it went there!* The infant perceives the relationship between objects in space and self. Memory is knowledge, and skill development becomes an essential ingredient in learning how to survive. Also, at this age, an infant can adapt to changing environments, which is a major determiner of intelligence and future learning situations.

18–24 months: A child at this age can invent new means of *internal combinations*. When an object is missing, he looks to find a replacement. The infant can remember where he left things or, better yet, remember what makes him happy, such as riding a tricycle or pushing a play shopping cart to stimulate movement. *Cause and effect* becomes an identity: *If I push the cart into the wall, it will go bang*, bringing much delight.

Brain Changing Note: Google Joseph Chilton Pearce, *Magical Child* (1977) and *Magical Child Matures* (1986).

Keys to Stimulate Cognition During the Sensory and Motor Stage

The following keys are taken from Huitt (1997):

Key #1: Baby Talk. Hang a cradle from your ceiling so you can talk and sing to your baby while you perform housework. If you cannot hang a cradle from the ceiling, then find your most comfortable chair and hold your baby while you read your favorite picture book. Point to pictures and be descriptive: *See the lion with the brown fur and long tail.* And always choose his favorite books before naptime. When reading a book, be aware of voice tones because, again, it stimulates the brain and bonding. When driving in a car, talk to the baby by pointing out traffic lights, road signs, and stores. When in a stroller have the child face you, if possible, so he can hear and see you as you describe what's happening on your walk.

Key #2: Have Fun With Your Baby. Have fun, fun, and more fun with your baby! Again, try to speak clearly and make eye contact. Don't be afraid to tell him what you're doing no matter how foolish you may feel or sound. When washing the dishes or simply making dinner, explain what you are doing. If you have a utensil in your hand, name it. The more you verbalize and vocalize in your particular voice, the more you stimulate the development of language as well as the brain.

Above all, make your sentences simple and not complex, and try to be energetic when you need to be and soft at other times.

Key #3: Mozart Would Have Loved This. There is so much research about how classical music (Mozart, Pachelbel, Bach) stimulates the brain. I always played a particular nature tape to my infant daughters before they went to bed each night. The sounds of waves or sounds of birds in a spring meadow are not only soothing but also stimulating. As your children grow older, choose fairy tales, and always keep the volume low.

Key #4: Toy Story. Choose toys that will stimulate their senses: touchy feely toys and mobiles, preferably those that are black and white, including black-and-white line designs. Find toys that make different sounds and manipulatives that are filled with holes and squares that the child can place objects through. Any object that the child can stack will work. Do not give the child too many objects to choose from, but try to keep the number to a minimum. When the child grows bored, present them with another toy, and so forth.

Stage 1: Preoperational, Toddlerhood to Early Childhood, Ages 2–7

At this *magical* stage, children's *imagination and intuition* become dominant in most learning situations. Moreover, their ability to use their intelligence to adapt and survive within their living environments is not only motivated by *sensory motor exploration* but also by the experience of *social interaction*. Through this experience, they can now reflect on the interactions with their caregivers as well as with other children.

This child is at *stage one cognitive thinking*, or the ability to entertain *one idea* at a time, which is usually a *highly egocentric view* of the world in which they live and play. The mantra at this age or stage is often *meeee!*

Their intelligence is expressed in the environments in which they live and play through *fantasy*. For example, the child playing with a toy sees the toy as alive and real, and the child gives the toy a name. Further, a moving toy car is alive even though the child is the one who is causing the car to move (Piaget called this realism). A doll might become your daughter's best friend, and the doll is not only alive but also has a particular personality. Further, Santa Claus and the Easter Bunny are real and alive.

Violent stories and words can be highly destructive, not only to the child's imagination but also to his emotional well-being. Further, violence, however imaginative, is still very real to a child at this stage, which is why parents need to monitor the child's television and movie viewing as well as their own arguments between themselves.

Further, this is a crucial period for the development and perception of the child's learning brain and school intelligence. Children who attach negative emotions to initial learning experiences could carry this perception of their intelligence for the rest of their lives. This is why preschools *must* integrate cognitive development theory into their teaching.

Brain Changing Note: Another example of the range of cognitive stages or delays can be observed on any kindergarten classroom wall with the different abilities in art and handwriting. For more, Google Dr. David Sortino, "Head Start: When a No Brainer Becomes a Brainer" and "School Readiness, Poverty, and Children's Brain Development."

Brain Changing Note: Joseph Pearce, author of *Magical Child* (1977) and *Magical Child Matures* (1986), discusses in his books how the *heart* plays a major role in the development of intelligence. According to Pearce, a nerve runs directly from the heart to the midbrain, the seat of cognition and emotion. When the heart is stimulated in a learning situation, the midbrain is stimulated as well. In short, the midbrain (limbic system) serves as a bridge to the old brain or cerebellum and new brain or the cerebral cortex, and greater intelligence or learning can take place. The statement "I learned it by heart" sums up Pearce's theory perfectly.

Examples of Preoperational Stage Thinking

Example #1: Coins in a Row. Show the child two rows of coins (rows A and B) and ask if the rows have the same number of coins.

Row A 0 0 0 0 0
Row B 0 0 0 0 0

Count for the child to show them that the two rows of coins have the same number of coins. Now separate the coins in row A and ask them which line has more coins.

Row A 0 0 0 0 0
Row B 0   0   0   0   0

Most children will say row B even if you have counted the coins. Again, the child sees the world *intuitively* and can only entertain *one idea at a time*, which is distance.

Example #2: Which Is Larger, the Sun or the Earth? Ask the child which is larger, the sun or earth, and they will say something like, "The earth . . . because it looks larger!" Again, at this stage, the child can only entertain one idea, which is *size*.

Example #3: First Grader's Reading Assignment. A first grader's homework reading assignment is for the parent and child to read one story before bedtime. The parent and child successfully read the story. However, the child still has ten minutes left before bedtime. The parent suggests they read another story, but the child refuses because *Teacher said to read only one story.* Although the parent tries to convince the child that the teacher would not mind if they read another story, the child is adamant and says, *No, teacher said to read only one story.*

So what's going on? The child's cognitive stage is limited to *stage one thinking*. He can entertain only one idea at a time or *can take the perspective of only one person*, which at this time is the teacher. If the mother interprets the child's refusal as disobedience, a struggle could ensue, and what had been a positive reading and learning experience could turn into something negative.

Further, the next time the child has a reading assignment, the child may only remember the previous negative reading experience with her mother rather than what could have been a totally positive learning experience. However, a few years later, the same child would not have any problem reading another story because she could now *entertain two perspectives—herself and the parent or teacher.*

Brain Changing Note: A major challenge for many children is learning how to read because of the multiple brain areas that are required to work together for a successful reading experience. Noted learning specialist and author Dr. David Sousa describes the complex reading process this way:

> Let's say reading begins with d-o-g. Next, the visual signals travel to the visual cortex located in the occipital lobe of the brain. The word d-o-g signals are decoded in an area of the left side of the brain called the angular gyrus, which separates it into basic sounds, or phonemes.
>
> The entire process activates the language brain areas located in the left hemisphere near and in the temporal lobe, where auditory processing occurs. The auditory processing system sounds out the phonemes in the head as in duh—awh—guh. Finally, Bronca's and Werneck's areas supply information about the word from their mental dictionaries, and the frontal lobe integrates

all the information to improve meaning—"a furry animal that barks." (Sousa, 2005)

Keys to Stimulate Stage One Thinking

The following keys are taken from Huitt (1997):

Key #1: Concrete Props. Use of concrete props and visual aides to illustrate lessons helps children understand what is being presented.

Key #2: Use Actions as Well as Words. This is where the importance of organization and structure comes in. Make instructions short and always try to use *animation/action* as well as words to eliminate the possibility that the child becomes confused. Also, action stimulates the child's multiple intelligences, which you will read about in chapter 2.

Key #3: Understanding the World. At this age, children are very egocentric because they can entertain only one perspective at a time, which is usually their own.

Key #4: Field Trips. Take field trips to zoos and parks and explore the habitats and animal life. Be sure to have children use all of their senses as they attempt to draw what they experienced.

Key #5: Manipulation of Objects. Encourage the manipulation of physical objects that can change in shape (clay, water, etc.) while still retaining a constant mass. Plan a visit to any Montessori or arts-oriented school for additional ideas.

Key #6: It's a Two-Way Street. Give children a chance to move toward the understanding of conversation and two-way logic needed for the next stage. Talk to your child using open-ended questions such as "What would be a good bedtime for children your age?"

Key #7: I Came, I Saw, I Touched. Use and teach words to describe what they are seeing, doing, touching, tasting, and smelling, since they all connect to the multiple learning intelligences. For example, lead a guided fantasy at the ocean, then have children research marine life of their choice and pretend what it must be like to live in the ocean.

Key #8: Show Differences. Use physical illustrations to show differences in size, shape, and so on. There are differences between objects of the same category, but we seldom take note or discuss these subtle deviations.

Key #9: Modeling and Then Some. After giving instructions, ask the child to demonstrate the instructions as a model for the rest of the class or to the family. Show fractions with children as in one out of twenty or half of a quantity. Use different colored items of clothing to teach grouping.

Key #10: It's All in the Game. Explain a game by acting out the parts of each participant.

Key #11: Mr. Rogers's Neighborhood. Avoid lessons about worlds too far removed from the child's experience. Choose local sites: home, neighborhood, school, village, town, city, county, state, country. Example: Have children draw a topo map of their home/neighborhood in relation to the school. Children can draw a map of their house, school, store, or church.

Key #12: Share and Share Alike. Discuss sharing from the child's own experience or point of view. Example: Describe all the different ways we share during the school day or at home, such as sharing art supplies, setting the table, washing dishes, and helping to prepare the meal.

Key #13: Alphabet Soup. Use cutout letters to build words. Again, Montessori schools use sandpaper letters to teach the alphabet by having children trace the letters with their fingers to stimulate their kinesthetic intelligence. Waldorf uses calligraphy to teach cursive writing. The simple kinesthetic, flowing movement of the pen on paper is said to stimulate higher sensory/motor skills.

Key #14: The Part Is Not Greater Than the Whole. Avoid overuse of workbooks and other paper-and-pencil tasks. Such items often operate as part-to-whole. You also need to teach whole-to-part to stimulate spatial intelligence and abstract thinking. If you were to teach the human body, you would show them the whole body first before teaching about the leg or head.

Key #15: Old Brain. Provide opportunities to play with clay, water, or sand. This is not only grounding but also stimulates the reptilian brain or cerebellum.

Key #16: Engagement. Engage students in conversations about the changes that each child or student is experiencing when manipulating objects. The more, the merrier!

Stage 2: Concrete Operational Thinking, Ages 7–11

> During the stage of concrete operational thinking (ages 7–11), a child's cognitive reasoning become logical. He develops what Piaget called logical operations. Piaget said that an intellectual operation is an internalized system of actions that is fully reversible. That is, the child exhibits logical thought processes (operations) that can be applied to problems that exist (concrete) and has no trouble solving problems and providing correct reasoning for his answer.
>
> When faced with a discrepancy between thought and perception, as in conservation problems, the concrete operational child makes cognitive and logical decisions as opposed to perceptual decisions. The child is no longer perception bound and becomes able—typically between the ages of 7 and 11—to do all the cognitive operations that limit the intellectual activity of the preoperational child. (Wadsworth, 1984)

The child now is older and more knowledgeable and can apply his knowledge to more challenging experiences and situations. Instead of only seeing the world intuitively and bounded by *egocentric perception*, he can now see the world concretely (black and white) and entertain *two ideas* at one time.

Brain Changing Note: "Usually around age 7 or 8 (the beginning of concrete operational stage of reasoning), children begin to grasp the significance of rules for proper game playing. Cooperation in a social sense begins to emerge. Rules are no longer seen as absolute and unchangeable. Children typically develop the notion that the rules of the game can be changed if all agree to the change. Children begin to try to win (a social act while conforming to the rules of the game" (Wadsworth, 1984).

Brain Changing Note: "Children would never learn rules to games if they didn't have *fun* playing the game" (Jean Piaget).

For example, a child knows that the sun is larger than the earth because the sun is far away. Hence, he not only can entertain the size of the earth but can also now use the perspective of distance: the sun is small because it is far away. The ability to entertain both sides of the coin is a major leap in his social or moral development.

Example #1: Conservation of Liquids. Two tall narrow beakers are filled with the same amount of water and another low wide beaker is left empty. Ask the child if beakers 1 and 2 have the same amount of water.

Next, pour the water from one of the tall beakers into the low and wide beaker 3 and ask if the taller beaker (2) has the same amount of water as the low and wide beaker.

Most six year olds will say the tall, thin beaker has more water, regardless of your having demonstrated that by pouring the water back into the taller beaker the amount of water was the same. Just as concrete operational children understand that the sun is larger than the earth (it only looks small because it is far away), the same principle can be applied to the water and beaker experiment.

At stage two (ages 7–11), children can accommodate (conserve) quantity and size or entertain two perspectives, while those children at the preoperational stage cannot.

Brain Changing Note: "Piaget would ask children the place on their body, if they had to put an extra eye, they would, [and] why they chose that place. Through this testing, Piaget found that children, starting about nine years old, would typically answer their third eye should be placed on the forehead. But children around eleven years old normally said their third eye should be put on their hand so they could see around corners! It is this characterization in their answer which indicates both abstract thinking and creative reasoning that is indicative of the next highest stage called formal operations" (Lockey, 2016).

Keys to Stimulate Stage Two Thinking

The following keys are taken from Huitt (1997):

Key #1: No One Ever Said It Was Going to Be Easy. Use concrete props like base ten blocks in mathematics or visual aids, especially when dealing with difficult material.

Key #2: Manipulating Geniuses. Give children the opportunity to manipulate objects to test out their ideas. Example: When teaching measurement, children need to use measuring sticks or rulers to measure the size of their classroom or bedroom.

Key #3: When You Keep It Simple, You Make It Simple. Make sure that discussions, readings, and instructions are brief and well organized, which is one strategy to keep lessons and learning potential organized.

Key #4: Life Is a Bowl of Variables. Ask students to deal with no more than three or more variables or ideas at a time.

Key #5: To Ponder Is to Think. Use familiar examples to help explain more complex ideas so that the child will have a beginning point for assimilating/acquiring new information. As should be the case with all our keys, we need to attach some emotional component to teaching. (See "The Bat Experiment" in the appendix.)

Key #6: The Organization Man. Provide opportunities to classify and group objects and ideas on increasingly complex levels. Create lessons that support abstract thinking examples, such as the bat experiment. (See "The Bat Experiment" in the appendix.)

Key #7: It Is as Plain as the Nose on Your Face. Present problems that require logical and analytical thinking to solve. Cooking and other practical experiences serve as good methods to encourage children to use logical and analytical thinking.

Key #8: History Will Repeat Itself. Provide timelines for history lessons and three-dimensional models in science. Start with the child's own *life script* or *timeline*, as well as family trees; if possible, use photos. In science, children can use manipulatives to construct models. The greater the learning, the greater the intelligence.

Key #9: Why Is the Sky Blue? Have all students participate in schoolwide scientific experiments. All schools should be required to conduct science fairs so that children can perform simple experiments, which may lead to more complex thinking.

Key #10: The Experimental Method. Illustrate daily occupations of people of an earlier period. If possible, children can work on their family's genealogy or family tree.

Key #11: The First Pilgrims. Have students read stories or books with short, logical chapters, moving to longer reading assignments, but only if the students are ready. Also, use serial books that employ the same characters but with different stories such as The Lord of the Ring, Harry Potter, and the like.

Key #12: Part-to-Whole. Conduct experiments with students that teach part-to-whole such as conservation of liquids; have older students conduct experiments with lower-grade students.

Key #13: Character Witness. Demonstrate experiments with a limited number of steps, like cooking a meal or painting the child's bedroom.

Key #14: Step-by-Step. Compare students' own lives with those of the characters in a story and then move on to the classics such as *Tom Sawyer*, *Huckleberry Finn*, and *Treasure Island*.

Key #15: I Could Have Been a Contender. Use story problems in math. Good examples include personal or consumer math for middle and high school students.

Key #16: One and One Is Three. Give students separate sentences on slips of paper to be grouped into paragraphs.

Key #17: Don't Give Me the Slip. Use outlines, hierarchies, and analogies to show the relationships of unknown material to already acquired knowledge such as predicting the weather and performing simple to more complex math and science problems.

Key #18: Whole-to-Part. Provide materials such as mind twisters, brain-teasers, and riddles. (See "The Bat Experiment" in the appendix.)

Key #19: Do You Mind. Focus discussions on open-ended questions that stimulate thinking: If London is in England and England is in Great Britain, is London in Great Britain?

Key #20: Ask This Question. Are the mind and the brain the same thing?

Key #21: Somewhere Over the Rainbow. Use stories that describe a culture living in harmony. Example: *Children Around the World* (DK Publishing, 1996).

Stage 3: Formal Operations, Ages 11 and older

At this stage, your student's problem-solving skills are becoming more sophisticated. Now he or she can entertain three or more perspectives (ideas) at one time. Whereas, the preoperational child is bounded by egocentric perception (entertain one perspective) and the concrete operational child is bounded by the concrete (two perspectives), the formal operational student is capable of a much broader range of logical thoughts. He can think in the future, and he is more advanced in conversation, which is why he questions adults and talks on his cell phone so often, because when he talks on the phone or talks back he is actually trying to *define himself*.

Brain Changing Note: "Adolescence is a time of significant growth and development inside the teenage brain. The main change is that unused connections in the thinking and processing part of your child's brain (called the grey matter) are pruned away. At the same time, other connections are strengthened. This is the brain's way of becoming more efficient, based on the 'use it or lose it' principle. This pruning process begins in the back of the brain. The front part of the brain, the prefrontal cortex, is remodeled last. The prefrontal cortex is the decision-making part of the brain, responsible for your child's ability to plan and think about the consequences of actions, solve problems and control impulses. Changes in this part continue into early adulthood" (Australia Department of Social Services 2017).

Brain Changing Note: Most brain scientists believe our brains grow to full size around the age of fourteen and are then capable of doing three-plus operations.

The student in stage three has the *potential* to deal with verbal complexities or abstract thinking, using trial and error to answer problems such as the following experiment with weights and string. Moreover, during this stage, the student becomes capable of looking within. Finally, he is capable of being independent about present, past, and future experiences and consequences: *If I drink and drive, I could end up seriously hurting someone.* Now they are capable of higher moral decision making.

Example 1: The Pendulum Problem. Ask two groups of children, ages seven to eleven, to explain what controls a pendulum's range of movement or oscillation. The problem is to isolate the length of the string from other factors to be considered by the children: the factors are the length of the string, the weight at the end of the string, the height from which the weight is dropped to start the motion, and the degree of force used to push the weight.

At the preoperational stage or, ages two to seven, most children believe that the pendulum's movement is dependent on how hard the child pushes it. At concrete operations, ages seven to eleven, children describe the relationship between the length of the pendulum's string and its movement, but they are unable to separate the other variables, such as weight and degree of force. They suspect that weight and push have something do with the movement, or back and forth motion.

The problem for this age group is that they are not able to reason that more than two factors (length of string, weight, and force) control the rate of movement. Conversely, the formal operational child has the potential to isolate *all the variables* present by looking at other factors, while still holding all factors equally. Notice how the following examples below, "The Bat Experiment" and "Two Girls at a Dance," describe similar results but with different variables or factors.

Example #2: The Bat Experiment (Reimer et al., 1990). Another experiment to distinguish between the different cognitive stages is to ask a group of ten- and eleven-year-olds to classify the following animals into groups:

Bat Cow Robin Hawk Dog

The majority of concrete operational students, ages seven to ten, would say *walking and flying* or *two legs or four legs*. They see the world logically and concretely, or from *two perspectives* at one time. However, a small percentage of this age group sees other categories. They know that a bat can fly yet it is also a mammal.

This group has the ability to see abstract categories or classify the groups by species. The ability to classify the group into species is a major step up from concrete operational thinking. Instead of entertaining *two ideas* at one time, they can entertain *three ideas* or formal operations. Teachers discover that even after they have taught the seven to ten age group about species, three to four weeks later those same students who are thinking at concrete operations tend to forget the more complex categories and still classify the animals as walking or flying.

Brain Changing Note: One teaching strategy a teacher employed with the bat experiment to raise her students' cognitive reasoning was to add a live bat to the lesson. Simply adding other intelligences (kinesthetic, visual, etc.) to the lesson helped stimulate the children's cognitive development to remember that bats must be categorized as a species and as such are mammals. That is, they have hair, give birth to their young (instead of laying eggs), and nurse their young. They do not have scales or feathers. They are warm-blooded and can regulate their own body temperature.

Note: After the teacher brought in a live bat to support the bat experiment, five weeks later the teacher tested the students again on classification of species, and 100 percent of the students classified bats as mammals (Sortino, 2019).

Example #3: Two Girls at a Dance. We can apply Piaget's cognitive theory to social situations as well. For example, two thirteen-year-old girls named Denise and Mary attend a dance, and both are interested in the same boy, whom we will call Peter. Denise has no problem asking Peter to dance, while Mary is hesitant.

From a cognitive perspective, Mary could end up losing the boy, not because of shyness but because her stage of cognitive thinking skills is formal operational. That is, Mary is hesitant about asking the boy to dance because she does not want the peer group to view her as someone who has *cut in* on Denise. Rather than being viewed by the peer group as *not nice*, she takes the high road and doesn't ask Peter to dance.

We would say that Mary's cognitive or thinking stage is formal operational because she can take the perspective of the group or three variables rather than simply satisfying her individual needs, like Denise. Conversely, Denise sees the world in *black and white* and can entertain only two ideas at one time, or Peter and Denise.

Of course, many factors could affect this example, but for children, and especially adolescents, such dilemmas are often an everyday experience. The problem with Denise's response is that when challenged to make (personal) moral decisions about more serious issues (sex, drugs, etc.), her personal needs could come first.

Conversely, Mary's moral reasoning takes in other factors, such as the group, which can represent the family, society, students, and more. In many ways, her judgment about serious issues will be group challenged. Unfortunately for Denise, if her moral/cognitive thinking is not challenged by the group, she may remain stuck at concrete operational thinking, which can seriously affect higher levels of moral reasoning resulting in potentially negative consequences (Reimer et al., 1990).

Example #4: Don't give me no lip! According to a news report, a certain private school in Cork, Ireland, was recently faced with a unique problem. A number of twelve-year-old girls were beginning to use lipstick and would put it on in the bathroom. That was fine, but after they put on their lipstick, they would press their lips to the mirror, leaving dozens of little lip prints.

Every night the custodian would remove them, and the next day the girls would put their lipstick prints back. Finally, the principal decided that something had to be done. She called all the girls and the custodian into the bathroom. She explained that all the lip prints were causing a major problem for the custodian who had to clean the mirrors every night.

To demonstrate how difficult it had been to clean the mirrors, she asked the maintenance man to show the girls how much effort was required. He took out a long-handled squeegee, dipped it in the toilet, and cleaned the mirror with it. Since then, there have been no lip prints on the mirror. *There are teachers and then there are teachers* .

Brain Changing Note: Raising a student's cognitive/moral development comes in all shapes and sizes. In our above example, the principal's discipline was not at stage two, black and white, or my way or the highway, but rather formal operational, or three ideas: the school, the custodian, and the girls.

Keys to Stimulate Stage Three Thinking

The following keys are taken from Huitt (1997):

Key #1: Like Death and Taxes. Ask students if one part of the test asks for answers that require more than rote memory. For example, essay questions might ask a student to justify two different positions on an issue. While discussing topics, ensure that the students consider more than one side of an issue.

Key #2: The Sun Never Sets on the British Empire. Give students an opportunity to explore hypothetical questions. Encourage students to explain how to solve problems. Use story diagrams.

Key #3: Broad Jumping. Whenever possible, teach broad concepts and not just facts, using materials and ideas relevant to the student. The world's population reached seven billion people in 2011. What effect will that have on food and countries with limited space? Example: Create a square on the classroom floor, six-by-six inches. Assuming the United States has one-seventh (300 million) of China's population (1.5 billion), have one student stand in one square. Now, create the same-sized square and have seven students stand in the square to illustrate what effect the different populations can have on space.

Key #4: A Picture Is Worth a Thousand Words. Use visual aids such as charts and illustrations, as well as simple but somewhat more sophisticated aids such as graphs and diagrams.

Key #5: One Step at a Time. Use well-organized materials that offer step-by-step explanations. Teach children to use checklists in their everyday school and home activities. For example, use whiteboards and large monthly calendars in their bedrooms to show important events, activities, and holidays.

Key #6: Social Intelligence. Don't leave home without it! Provide students opportunities to discuss social issues. Break students up into small groups and assign one student to be the leader. Rotate the leaders on a weekly basis.

Key #7: ET Phone Home. Provide consideration of a hypothetical other world or contemplate what is meant by infinity.

Key #8: Me, Myself, and I. Ask students to work in pairs, with one student acting as the problem solver, thinking out loud while tackling a problem, and the other student acting as the listener, checking to see that all steps are mentioned and that everything seems logical.

Key #9: The Times They Are a-Changin'. Use lyrics from music to teach poetic devices to reflect social problems, such as Bob Dylan's song "The Times They Are a-Changin'."

Chapter Two

Multiple Intelligence

Identifying Your Child's True Intelligence
— Dr. Howard Gardner (1943–)

A young girl spends an hour with an examiner. She is asked a number of questions that probe her store of information (Who discovered America? What does the stomach do?), her vocabulary (What does nonsense mean?, What does belfry mean?), her arithmetic skills (At eight cents each how much will three candy bars cost?), her ability to remember a series of numbers (5, 1, 7, 4, 2, 3, 8), her capacity to grasp the similarity between two elements (elbows and knee, mountain and lake).

She may also be asked to carry out certain other tasks—the girl's intelligence quotient or IQ. This number (which the little girl may actually be told) is likely to exert appreciable effect upon her future, influencing the way in which her teacher thinks of her and determining her eligibility for privileges. The importance attached to her number is not entirely inappropriate: After all, the score on an intelligence test does predict one's ability to handle school, though it foretells little of success in late life.

In my view, if we are to encompass adequately the realm of human cognition, it is necessary to include a far wider and more universal set of competences than we have ordinarily considered. And it is necessary to remain open to the possibility that many—if not most—of these competences do no lend themselves to measurement by standard verbal methods, which rely heavily on blend of logical and linguistic abilities. (Gardner, 1983)

Howard Earl Gardner is an American developmental psychologist and the John H. and Elisabeth A. Hobbs Professor of Cognition and Education at the

Harvard University Graduate School of Education. He is noteworthy for developing the concept of *multiple intelligences*, eight different modalities of learning that we all fall into to greater or lesser degrees.

Brain Changing Note: Recently, a ninth intelligence has been suggested: "There are many people who feel that there should be a ninth intelligence, *existential intelligence* (a.k.a.: "wondering smart, cosmic smart, spiritually smart, or metaphysical intelligence"). The possibility of this intelligence has been alluded to by Howard Gardner in several of his works. He has stated that existential intelligence might be manifest in someone who is concerned with fundamental questions about existence, or who questions the intricacies of existence. And while Professor Gardner has offered a preliminary definition as: 'Individuals who exhibit the proclivity to pose and ponder questions about life, death, and ultimate realities,' he has not fully confirmed, endorsed, or described this intelligence" (Wilson, 2018b). For more, Google Dr. David Sortino, "When IQ Tests Take Precedent Over True Intelligence."

Beyond the eight intelligences discussed in this chapter, such as the mathematical and the linguistic, there are other intelligences that not only support the brain changing concept but also can stimulate higher learning levels. Parents and educators need to research alternative schools and programs that acknowledge and integrate multiple intelligence *into their school curriculums*. Again, a good example of school programs that integrate multiple intelligence are Waldorf and Montessori schools or arts-centered programs or schools.

Dr. Maria Montessori created a school program for orphaned children who exhibited attachment disorders (caused by lack of touching, bonding, etc.). Montessori's school curriculum centered on stimulating the children's kinesthetic intelligence by addressing the areas of the brain (cerebellum, limbic system) that had suffered from a want of a mother's touch? Again, one Montessori strategy employed sandpaper letters to stimulate areas of the brain associated with the alphabet or phonemic awareness to support reading development. Further, Waldorf schools (based on the ideas of Rudolf Steiner) integrate the arts, music, dance, calligraphy, drama, and more as an essential ingredient for higher-order learning, further reinforcing the multiple intelligence philosophy.

Brain Changing Note: "Children learn best when connections are made with their brain through their senses, a fact that has heavily influenced Montessori classrooms' approach to education. This means listening to a lesson only uses hearing, limiting the possible connections with the content. A lack of real-world connection can make information harder to understand, memorize, and use. However, if they are encouraged to make noises or create a *Play-dog pig* instead of just repeating the name, they are forming more connections and assigning further meaning to the lesson" (Montessori Kids Brandon, 2017).

Brain Changer: Maria Tecla Artemisia Montessori (1870–1952) was an Italian physician and educator best known for the philosophy of education that bears her name and for her writing on scientific pedagogy. Google Dr. Maria Montessori for additional information.

Brain Changing Note: Take a multiple intelligence assessment for a better understanding of Gardner's eight multiple intelligence types before reading this chapter. Search the internet for free multiple intelligence assessments. A typical assessment asks around twenty-four questions and will take less than five minutes to complete. Try not to think too hard—just go with your first thought when describing your daily activities and interests. By the end, you may have some new insights into how you think as well as how your students or children think.

LINGUISTIC INTELLIGENCE

> The roots of spoken language can be found in the child's babbling during the opening months of life. Indeed, even deaf youngsters begin to babble early in life, and during the first months, all infants will issue those sounds found in linguistic stocks remote from their home tongue. (Gardner, 1983)

Words, words, and more words! Children with a strong linguistic intelligence are the early talkers and wordsmiths of the human world! As young infants, you can hear them babbling until the late hours of the night. As toddlers, they will begin to talk early and, to your amazement, never stop talking right up until leaving home for college! They are filled with *why* questions and are fiercely argumentative simply because this is what they do best. In short, they would never miss a chance to question you or start a good argument or discussion, particularly during adolescence.

Furthermore, you will often hear young toddlers alone in their rooms, simply talking to themselves or communicating to an imaginary friend, toy car, or doll. This is simply how their brains express the *magical child's stage of linguistic intelligence.*

Brain Changing Note: "When I was a child, my parents' fights could suck the oxygen out of a room. My mother verbally lashed out at my father, broke jam jars, and made outlandish threats. Her outbursts froze me in my tracks. When my father fled to work, the garage, or the woods, I felt unprotected. Years later, when my husband and I decided to have children, I resolved never to fight in front of them" (Developmental Education, 2014).

The sagacious teacher should take advantage of this child's linguistic skills by letting them help with classroom activities such as attendance or lunch count, as well as have them work in primary classrooms reading to younger children. In addition, teachers need to seat these children in front of the class because they need to talk, discuss, and just be heard; otherwise, they can become disruptive by disturbing other children and labeled as a potential behavior problem.

At an early age, Johnny Carson studied magic so that he could perform tricks at birthday parties. It was not so much the magic tricks but that he simply needed a diversion from shyness to talk in front of groups.

Parents can provide the linguistic child with an audio recorder so he can create and hear himself. In addition, such children will want to listen to audio stories before bedtime with the lights off, stimulating their imagination to reach new heights. When such children get older, they can create their own radio shows and may want to interview you and other family members.

Brain Changing Note: As a child, John Miller, Hall of Fame baseball announcer, would sit in the center field bleachers at Candlestick Park with a tape recorder and announce the San Francisco Giants baseball games years before he became a professional broadcaster.

These children almost always possess all other linguistic abilities, such as writing or oral reading. Allow time in the classroom for these students to keep a journal, which someday could turn into a book. Play reading can take center stage with this personality as well.

With study skills, they need to keep notes or verbalize to themselves or teach others what they have just learned or are about to learn. (See "Pyramid of Learning" in the appendix.)

In addition, buy them a good dictionary, thesaurus, or encyclopedia, and leave them alone as they explore the world of words and verbal information. Be sure to always set up a time for them to discuss the information with you. The Achilles' heel for this child is that they will most likely fall in love with the internet, cell phones, and other technology in their need to communicate.

Brain Changing Note: See Sirkin (2013) on how to build a crystal radio—plus how they work.

In high school, students can volunteer at the local radio or TV station. Further, they will be attracted to the school's debate team, yearbook, literature club, or anything associated with linguistic self-expression.

Careers associated with communication and writing include being a teacher, writer, speech instructor, actor, or anything associated with TV and radio. From the local car salesmen who just made you *the best deal of your life* to the Sunday preacher, the world of communication is theirs if they follow their linguistic intelligence truthfully. These linguistic learners relish a life of verbal self-expression and creativity!

Using your knowledge of linguistic intelligence, describe any unique behaviors your child has exhibited in the following areas:

- Activities such as storytelling, reading, or imaginary play
- Homework/study skills such as note taking or creating a school schedule
- Play/activities such as play reading or building a crystal radio
- School interests or activities such as school newspaper, yearbook, or drama club
- Careers spoken about or demonstrated interests such as newspaper editor, journalism, radio/TV announcer, or sales

For more ideas, Google "Study Tips Based on Multiple Intelligence (How You Learn)."

LOGICAL–MATHEMATICAL INTELLIGENCE

> It is undeniable that a gift for math is often a most specialized talent and that mathematicians as a class are not particularly distinguished for general ability or versatility. If man is in any sense a real mathematician, then it is hundred to one that his math will be better than anything else he can do and . . . he would be silly if he surrenders a decent opportunity of exercising his one talent in order to do an undistinguished work in other fields. (G. H. Hardy, quoted in Gardner, 1983)

As infants, children with logical–mathematical intelligence could become frustrated with disorganization because they prefer predictability or what is logical, which is often due to their dominant linear or mathematical left brains. Therefore, parents should always maintain a predictable schedule for these young children. In other words, such children live in a *logical/sequential* world in which their analytical minds could become impatient with illogical or disorganized energy or behavior. As is the case with all infants, use lots of pictures (solar system) on the ceilings above their cribs to stimulate their spatial intelligence (the brain's right side) to balance out the brain's left side.

These children should be able to count before they can walk, and they will gravitate to most anything that promotes the linear world of numbers and logic. They can complete numbered dot-to-dot books at the earliest of age. Further, they love puzzles, using their kinesthetic intelligence to attach the puzzle pieces in a logical order.

In early childhood, math workbooks could occupy their linear or sequential thinking brains and entertain them for about a minute, and then they will need to move on to more sophisticated analytical mind games or brain teasers. When presented with a movable toy, they would rather take it apart to see how it works.

Brain Changing Note: "Little children are naturally attracted to the science of number. Mathematics, like language, is the product of the human intellect. It is therefore part of the nature of a human being. Mathematics arises from the human mind as it comes into contact with the world and as it contemplates the universe and the factors of time and space. It undergirds the effort of the human to understand the world in which he/she lives. All humans exhibit this mathematical propensity, even little children. It can therefore be said that human kind has a mathematical mind" (Association Montessori International of the United States, 2017).

They will begin asking for a computer before they begin kindergarten. When you take them on hikes, you might see them counting the number of steps it takes to get to the store, to get home, or the number of steps to their bedroom. When you shop, don't be surprised if they try to figure out the bill before you get to the checkout counter or question you when you buy one item for three dollars when you can get two items for five! Their brains want to operate in the linear-logical-numerical world, so be prepared for them to play board games, checkers, and especially chess at an early age.

Again, Montessori, Steiner, and the International Baccalaureate are excellent school programs because they allow students to experience classification and comparison of how all life elements (mathematically and scientifically) fit into the real world.

Brain Changer: Rudolf Joseph Lorenz Steiner (1861–1925) was an Austrian philosopher, social reformer, architect, and esotericist. Steiner gained initial recognition at the end of the nineteenth century as a literary critic and published philosophical works, including *The Philosophy of Freedom*. Google Rudolf Steiner for additional information.

Brain Changing Note: Founded in 1968, the International Baccalaureate (IB) is a nonprofit educational foundation offering four highly respected programs of international education that develop the intellectual, personal, emotional, and social skills needed to live, learn, and work in a rapidly globalizing world.

As these children move into late childhood, you will notice that they are collectors, so expect their rooms to be filled with anything from rocks to bottle caps. Again, they live in a logical or linear world and will ask you a million *whys*, so be sure you know what you are talking about because they will hold you to it and remind you of your mistakes every chance they get.

In elementary school, they are the math brains or nerds. Therefore, don't be alarmed if everything goes to pot, like Cs and Ds in English and history, but always an A+ in math!

Moreover, they will be head and shoulders over most students in math classes, and the teachers could end up having to find ways to individualize their math lessons. It is not unusual for them to be sent next door to work at a higher math grade level.

Also, it might be time to bring in a math tutor to keep them motivated or to enroll them in intensive summer math camps and programs that allow them to use their math skills in creative ways such as coding, robotic technology, or computer programming.

In high school, they should join math clubs and hang out with other math "nerds." But beware: this group has a tendency to move on to other *worlds*, and often their social skills are neglected because math and numbers are addictive to their learning brains. In short, this behavior can isolate them with other math junkies who see the world in the same vein.

Brain Changing Note: Students who are talented in mathematics often demonstrate an uneven pattern of mathematical understanding and development since some are much stronger in *concept development* than they are in *computation* (Rotigel & Lupkowski-Shoplik 1999; Sheffield, 1994).

There are universities such as MIT and Cal Tech that can train these math learners in such careers as aerospace, computer science, astronomy, and more. In summary, it is hoped that these careers will lead to mathematical self-actualization and a sense of personal fulfillment.

Gifted math students often want to know more about the hows and whys of mathematical ideas than the computational how-to processes (Sheffield, 1994). Since these children often prefer to learn all they can about a particular mathematical idea before leaving it for new concepts, a more expansive approach to mathematics based on student interest may avoid the frustration that occurs when the regular classroom schedule demands moving on to another topic.

Brain Changing Note: "Any opportunity you can give students to answer math and logic problems, look for patterns, organize items and solve even simple science problems can help them boost their logical-mathematical intelligence" (Kelly, 2017).

A more linear approach to mathematics is often a better match for gifted children instead of the spiral curricula often found in textbook series and followed by classroom teachers. For example, when the topic of decimals is introduced, children with mathematical talent should be allowed to delve much further into the topic, learning practical applications for decimals and the connections between decimals and other mathematical topics (Rotigel & Lupkowski-Shoplik, 1999).

Using your knowledge of mathematical–logical intelligence, describe any unique behaviors your child has exhibited in the following areas:

- Activities associated with problem solving, particularly with numbers
- Homework/study skills that include counting, measuring, or graphing
- Play/activities including chess, checkers, or map reading
- School interests or activities that include computer classes, math clubs, astronomy, or rocketry
- Careers spoken about or demonstrated interests including engineering, drafting, or architecture

For more ideas, Google "Study Tips Based on Multiple Intelligence (How You Learn)."

SPATIAL INTELLIGENCE

Central to spatial intelligence are the capacities to perceive the visual world accurately, to perform transformations and modifications upon one's initial perceptions, and to be able to re-create aspects of one's visual experience, even in the absence of relevant physical stimulation. (Gardner, 1983)

The infant in the crib with the far-off, quiet look in his eyes could be exhibiting his or her spatial intelligence by seeing designs, abstractions, and colors on his bedroom's walls and ceiling.

Brain Changing Note: Gardner (1983) explains, "at the end of the sensory-motor stage of early childhood, youngsters become capable of mental imagery. They can imagine a scene or an event without having to be there."

Brain Changing Note: There is even evidence that early spatial ability predicts a young child's readings skills (Franceschini, Gori, Ruffino, Pedrolli, & Facoetti, 2012).

Brain Changing Note: Many studies have found that high visual-spatial ability is linked to better math performance. A one-million-dollar pilot project supported by the National Institute of Child Health and Human Development shows how improving spatial thinking can result in better math skills.

In this project, kindergarteners and first graders were randomly assigned to two after-school intervention groups. In one group, children were asked to construct and copy designs made from a variety of materials such as Legos, pattern blocks, and construction papers. The control group, on the other hand, was given a nonspatial curriculum. After about seven months, the children in the first group made a substantial improvement in their math performance. They moved from the thirtieth percentile nationwide in numeracy and applied math knowledge to the forty-seventh percentile. In the control group, no gain in math score was observed (Sparks, 2013).

Moreover, children with a propensity toward spatial intelligence see the world differently: a cloud can become a magic theater in the sky. As young children, they can produce the most wonderful designs, blending in various shapes and colors. In school, they need to visualize the lesson first before the teacher verbalizes it, or better yet, they will respond well to show-and-tell instruction. They are capable of seeing abstractions inside of abstractions!

When creating homework exercises, you might want to color code the different assignments. Further, when they are reading or doing math assignments, you need to be sure to reinforce the *sequential* since their brains will almost always want to go to the abstract/spatial or nonverbal and be drawn to the whole rather than to the part. In class, they could have auditory processing problems listening to lectures since their brains automatically want to visualize the big picture rather than to automatically sequence the world at large. Therefore, be sure to seat them in the front of the room and reconnect verbally, by a touch on the shoulder, or with eye contact as often as possible.

Brain Changing Note: Young children who are better at visualizing spatial relationships develop stronger arithmetic abilities in primary school (Zhang et al., 2012).

In addition, as a teacher or parent, you might have to pull these students aside and help them sequence what you just said in a way that does not come across as negative or condescending. However, the more they can sequence, the better they will do in school, especially in skill development. In addition, some children will begin to sight read and become voracious readers well ahead of other children because they can mentally *see* and *remember* the entire word or read whole-to-part. For others, they could have difficulties when they attempt whole-to-part reading because their brains are not ready to make this transition, and instead they need to break the word up into parts for better comprehension.

Brain Changing Note: One of the greatest problems confronting early readers is that 50 percent of English words have *silent letters*, which can cause reading delays. Too often, such children are identified with a learning disability when, in fact, it is only because they experience the world of reading spatially. So parents need to be patient but also teach them to decode or break up words into parts to reinforce phonics and encourage decoding skills.

At home, when you give verbal directions, have the child repeat the directions back to you, but again not in a way that seems to be corrective. They see the end result first and like to process whole-to-part when school lessons teach part-to-whole. Place white boards in their rooms or large monthly schedules in main home activity or traffic areas so that they can visually clue in on daily reminders. Such tools will help them focus on important school events and homework dates as well as help them realize that the world is very linear, left-brain, and sequential.

In middle school, if they have developed the skills to conceptualize what they have learned, they often become excellent students because they are able to think abstractly (formal operations) or out of the box. Again, with study skills, such children need to see learning from a visual perspective by color coding important words or assignments. Furthermore, when writing a term paper or essay, they can construct story maps or story wheels to outline their thoughts on paper

Brain Changing Note: Google Dr. David Sortino, "Transitioning to Middle-School."

Brain Changing Note: Google "How to Construct a Story Map."

Brain Changing Note: In high school, parents can begin to register their student in junior college summer classes or involve them in volunteer work that supports the arts or their spatial abilities, such as astronomy, digital design, and more.

In college, the sky is the limit for such learners, as they will continue their interests and pursue the many choices of design, geography, photography, architecture, and advertising.

Brain Changing Note: "Central to spatial intelligence are the capacities to perceive the visual world accurately, to perform transformations and modifications upon one's initial perceptions, and to be able to re-create aspects of one's visual experiences, even in the absence of relevant physical stimuli" (Gardner, 1983).

They can pursue civil enterprises and become urban planners or follow their visual interests in environmental studies. If they have a bent toward the kinesthetic, they can apply their spatial intelligence to landscape design, architecture, air traffic control, dance and film, and scene design and editing.

Brain Changing Note: A good spelling/reading strategy that parents can employ is called the Auditory Discrimination in Depth Program (ADD), created by authors Charles and Patricia Lindamood (1975). The program teaches children to use sound and symbol in conjunction with the three senses: hearing, seeing, and feeling.

Using your knowledge of spatial intelligence, describe any unique behaviors or interests associated with your child.

- Activities such as arts and crafts, map making, astronomy, or graphic design
- Homework/study skills such as learning story maps, graphs, or the five-paragraph essay
- Play/activities such as photography, art classes, or graphic design
- School interests or activities such as graphic design or map reading
- Careers spoken about or demonstrated interests such as interior designer, architect, or landscape design

For more ideas, Google "Study Tips Based on Multiple Intelligence (How You Learn)."

KINESTHETIC INTELLIGENCE

The essential requirement of any performance that can be called skilled becomes much plainer if we look at a few actual instances: a player in a quick ball game; the operator engaged at his workbench directing his machine and using his tools; the surgeon conducting another operation; the physician arriving at a clinical decision. In all these instances and in innumerable other ones that could just as well be used, there is the continuing flow from signals occurring outside the performance as interpreted by him to actions carried out; then, onto further signals and more action, up to the culmination point of the achievement of the task or whatever part of the task is the immediate objective. . . . Skilled persons must at all times submit to the receptor control, and must be initiated and directed by the signals which the performance needs to pick up from his environment, in combination with the signal, internal to his own body, which will tell him about his own movements as he makes them. (Sir Frederic Bartlett, quoted in Gardner, 1993).

Children with an inclination toward a *kinesthetic intelligence* are the physical movers and shakers of the multiple intelligence world! At age three, my parents attached a harness to a fifteen-foot rope and connected the rope to a tree to prevent me from climbing over our six-foot fence and escaping. In fact, I became so expert in my escapes, the local police department began calling me by my first name! Today I would be drugged, flogged, and labeled ADHD (attention deficit hyperactivity disorder), and who knows in what SED (seriously emotionally disturbed) program I would have been placed!

Brain Changing Note: Google Dr. David Sortino, "Look Before You Leap: Identifying ADD and ADHD Children."

We need to recognize that such children are not being rebellious but only displaying their kinesthetic intelligence and their need to express this intelligence physically or with their bodies. As young babies, they need to entertain themselves while in the crib. Therefore, hang mobiles and other kinesthetic sensory or visual stimuli.

When they get older and move out of the crib, they will need space to move safely. Therefore, child proof your home! Remember, it is not only their bodies that are moving in a hundred different directions, but also their brain (kinesthetic intelligence) that is trying to figure out ways to move and escape as well!

As they move up the kinesthetic ladder, they need contraptions like Johnny Jump Ups (those contraptions that hang from the doorway). Moreover, they will try to begin walking sooner than most, so you should purchase a toy shopping cart as a way to give them the training wheels to move around.

Brain Changing Note: "Many educators have had the experience of not being able to reach some students until presenting the information in a completely different way or providing new options for student expression. Perhaps it was a student who struggled with writing until the teacher provided the option to create a graphic story, which blossomed into a beautiful and complex narrative. Or maybe it was a student who just couldn't seem to grasp fractions, until he created them by separating oranges into slices" (Edutopia, 2016a).

At preschool, teachers will have to take note of this child and be sensitive to his need for periodic breaks. In circle time, this child should sit close to teachers or on the periphery so that he can stretch and move. Do not put two kinesthetic children together, for their energies will feed into each other, and instead of one energetic child you will get two times two, and a circle group will become several chaotic groups. Such children should participate in continuous-movement sports, such as soccer, cross-country, or basketball, because they allow their bodies to keep moving.

In elementary school, these children need to express their learning with their bodies. They do especially well in science when they can move about creating a science project, and of course they do well in PE, music, and art. Montessori is a wonderful school program for this child for reasons I have already mentioned.

Brain Changing Note: "Traditionally, schools have addressed bodily intelligence through recess, physical education, and participation in sports programs (Gardner, 1993). The Council on Physical Education for Children (COPEC) strongly supports daily physical education and recess. Unfortunately, daily participation in these activities is quite limited in contemporary American school life, and many schools are not following the COPEC guidelines. In some programs, recess has been eliminated to provide more instructional time. Physical education might only occur once a week.

"In addition, organized sports have become very stressful and demanding for children. In many programs there is little time, if any, provided for creative use of the body, for children to create games or projects, or engage in movement without the intervention or direction of an adult. While schools have addressed the purely physical aspects of movement, the bodily realm also includes emotional expression, role-play, games, and bodily expression of thoughts, ideas, and information" (Hirsh, 2010).

Further, in the classroom or at home, you should let them act out stories that you have read. When teaching, make physical contact with them by addressing them with a hand on the shoulder when they get antsy (be aware of the ten minutes rule for each grade level).

Brain Changing Note: Kinesthetic and tactile learners have difficulty learning steps and procedures. Tip: Teach kinesthetic learners to visualize themselves doing what they are learning. If you are teaching them steps for solving a problem, have them go inside their imaginations and *see* themselves following the steps (Child First, 2016).

Another excellent strategy for children who have difficulty sitting at a desk for long periods of time is to allow this student to sit on a *swivel seat* to address their fidgeting needs. Also, create a few *elevated desks* that allow the student to stand.

Also, this child can use dance and theater for greater self-expression as a link to their musical intelligence. By the time they reach middle school, if your student is still having difficulties focusing in the classroom, consider a learning or occupational specialist for additional suggestions. By the time they reach high school, these kinesthetic learners should have less of a problem (hopefully) due to the current popularity of multiple intelligence teaching strategies.

Brain Changing Note: Parents can contact their high school counselor for appropriate support, which could include vocational and occupational assessments.

In addition, all sports, whether individual or group oriented, are beneficial. Moreover, parents should be aware of two other intelligences called the *intrapersonal* and the *interpersonal* when selecting individual versus group sports. For example, the child with a preferred *intrapersonal intelligence* is more reticent and often prefers individual sports and activities rather than team sports, whereas the child with a preferred *interpersonal intelligence* gravitates to team sports and actually could feel comfortable competing in front of crowds.

College studies should encompass some aspects of the arts, recreation, and athletics. The future careers of kinesthetic learners should be associated with movement because they are experts at expressing their bodily intelligences and, most importantly, can walk the walk and talk the talk. I started out as a PE teacher and moved on to other areas of teaching. Any success I had teaching at-risk students could be attributed to my knowledge regarding my own kinesthetic needs for short breaks and activities that support the need to express anger or anxiety through movement. In short, I applied my strong PE, sports, and kinesthetic intelligence to help at-risk students channel their anger physically in a more positive way through such activities.

Lastly, children gifted in kinesthetic intelligence could become excellent PE teachers, coaches, dancers, and even brain surgeons! Just writing about them tires me out!

Brain Changing Note: Google Dr. David Sortino, *The Promised Cookie: No Longer Angry Children* (2011).

Using your knowledge of kinesthetic intelligence, describe any unique behaviors your child exhibits in the following areas:

- Activities including all individual and team sports
- Homework/study skills that includes pictorial graphs or organizational charts
- Play/activities including biking, hiking, or building forts
- School interests or recreational activities including all sport and physical activities in general
- Careers spoken about or demonstrated interests such as coach, personal trainer, or sport's writer

For more ideas, Google "Study Tips Based on Multiple Intelligence (How You Learn)."

MUSICAL INTELLIGENCE

> Of all the gifts with which individuals may be endowed, none emerges earlier than musical talent. Though speculation on this matter has been rife, it remains uncertain just why musical talent emerges so early and what the nature of this gift might be. A study of musical intelligence may help us understand the special flavor of music and, at the same time, illuminate its relation to other forms of human intellect. (Gardner, 1983)

If you hear your child cooing quietly in his crib, he could be displaying Gardner's musical or linguistic intelligences. Therefore, it might be time to hang a musical mobile above the crib, playing some short ditty like "Twinkle, Twinkle, Little Star" or even better Pachelbel's Canon in D.

Brain Changing Note: "The Mozart Effect was first suggested by a scientific study published in 1993 in the respected *Journal of Science*. It showed that teenagers who listened to Mozart's 1781 Sonata for Two Pianos in D major performed better in reasoning tests than adolescents who listened to something else or who had been in a silent room. The study (which did not look at the effect of Mozart on babies) found that college students who listened to a Mozart sonata for a few minutes before taking a test that measured spatial relationship skills did better than students who took the test after listening to another musician or no music at all" (*Telegraph Reporter*, 2015).

Furthermore, one must not forget that music is related to the other intelligences, which is why parents need to be aware of the kinesthetic (dance) and linguistic (choral) intelligences expressing themselves jointly or early. For example, various primitive tribes teach or require children to begin to express their emotions in dance or words.

Gardner (1983) writes, "Once one casts a comparative glance around the globe, a far wider variety of musical trajectories becomes manifest. At one extreme are the Anan of Nigeria. Infants scarcely a week old are introduced to music and dancing by their mothers. Fathers fashion small drums for their children. When they reach the age of two, children join groups where they learn many basic cultural skills, including singing, dancing, and playing instruments."

Brain Changing Note: "A new type of neuron—called a *mirror neuron*—could help explain how we learn through mimicry and why we empathize with others. . . . Mirror neurons are a type of brain cell that respond equally when we perform an action and when we witness someone else perform the same action" (Winerman, 2005).

Also, play and speak nursery rhymes with your child. Let them pound on pots and pans or whatever is appropriate to express rhythm and sound to stimulate the kinesthetic or linguistic intelligences.

Brain Changing Note: "Seeing is doing—at least it is when mirror neurons are working normally. But in autistic individuals, say researchers from the University of California, San Diego, the brain circuits that enable people to perceive and understand the actions of others do not behave in the usual way" (University of California–San Diego, 2005).

As they grow older, they can learn the difficult math facts (times tables) by singing and tapping them in time or by jumping rope. You will be surprised how quickly children can master math facts because singing and movement is connected to the cerebellum and the child's kinesthetic intelligence.

Brain Changing Note: "When we realize that because of its coordinating function, the cerebellum is intrinsically tied to timing, rhythm and sequencing, it will come as no surprise that learning is easier when we include rhythm and rhyme. Have you noticed how much easier it is to learn the words of a poem or song than learning simple text? When we learn our 'times tables' we rely on the rhythm and (admittedly not a very melodic) melody.

"If you have taught children their 'times tables' you have noticed that when you ask them 'what is 3x6' they will silently speed through the 'song' of the times table until they reach it. While this does not impart meaning to the numbers, it allowed for easier learning and easier retrieval and I have used this in helping children increase their repertoires of 'sight words' when learning to read" (Stansfield, 2012).

For reading classes, children can sing phrases or write their own songs and learn simple jingles. Always try to expose them to different kinds of music such as rock, folk, classical, and opera to stimulate the higher brain centers with musical intelligence. The window of opportunity for music begins at three and closes about ten (Sousa, 2005).

As these children move out of infancy and toddlerhood and into early childhood, parents could enlist a teacher schooled in the Suzuki method—a good option for this age group. Two important factors separate the Suzuki method from other methods. First, the Suzuki method believes that children should start playing as soon as they can hold a violin, and second, the child is taught to *intuit* the playing of the violin.

Brain Changing Note: Beginning in third grade, Waldorf students are required to play a stringed instrument for at least three years. Prior to third grade, children are required to play the recorder.

Brain Changing Note: "The right brain is the location of your intuition. Emotions, senses, music, art, and creative thought are right-brain experiences. Many people get so use to just focusing on left-brain functions that they forget to give the right brain a chance to be heard.

Are you too busy to have some creative fun? Do you make time to listen to music, sit quietly, and breathe? You can experience right-brain intuition when the left brain takes a break. But quieting your mind is just part of the process. Lots of people tend to dismiss intuitive information when they recognize it, because it seems so out of sync with logic. But it is real" (Langholt, 2017).

Late childhood could see the assent into musical groups or a school orchestra. If they attend a school that lacks a music program, consult your local symphony for qualified teachers.

Brain Changing Note: "Learning to play a musical instrument relies on understanding concepts, such as fractions and ratios, that are important for mathematical achievement." (Gaab & Zuk, 2017).

By the time your student begins high school, they will be on their way to expressing their musical interests in a variety of ways with the school orchestra or by starting their own musical group. The end result could be a potential career in one of the many other areas of musical expression.

Brain Changing Note: "The Beatles were the most innovative, emulated, and successful music group of the twentieth century. The Beatles set in motion both the creative and marketing paradigms of the modern rock era—

through transforming hairstyles and fashion; evolving attitudes about youth, politics, and drug culture; writing their own songs and making the first music videos to accompany them; performing the first arena rock concerts; creating the first unified rock albums alongside hit singles; and being the first rock performers who were truly considered groundbreaking artists in their own time" (Encyclopedia.com, 2018).

In addition, there are many other musical vocational directions to choose from. They could become a sound mixer, media tech, or radio technician. The list is endless. Always remember that musical intelligence is an excellent support for other intelligences as well.

Using your knowledge of musical intelligence, describe any unique behaviors your child exhibits in the following areas:

- Activities such as singing, dance, or playing an instrument
- Homework/study skills such as learning the times tables by tapping feet or singing
- Play/activities such as humming, singing, dancing, or playing an instrument
- School interests or activities associated with band, choral, or dance
- Careers spoken about or demonstrated interests as a musician, dancer, singer, or sound mixer

For more ideas, Google "Study Tips Based on Multiple Intelligence (How You Learn)."

INTERPERSONAL INTELLIGENCE

Interpersonal intelligence is the ability to notice and make distinctions among other individuals and, in particular, among their moods, temperaments, motivations, and intuitions. Examined in its most elementary form, interpersonal intelligence entails the capacity of the young child to discriminate among the individuals around him and to detect their various moods.

In an advanced form, interpersonal knowledge permits a skilled adult to read the intuitions and desires—even when these have been hidden in many other individuals, and potentially to act upon its knowledge, such as by influencing a group of disparate individuals to behave along desired lines.

We see highly developed forms of interpersonal intelligence in political and religious leaders (Mahatma Gandhi or John F. Kennedy), in skilled parents and teachers, and in individuals enrolled in the helping professions such as therapists, counselors, or shamans. (Gardner, 1983)

They are the young infants who seem to make eye contact as soon as they come out of the womb. They might be those children who need constant attention, so be sure to engage them in conversation and social interaction. You can hang a cradle from the ceiling in the middle of your house so you can always talk to your baby. In strollers, the child should *face the parent* so that he is part of a social activity.

Brain Changing Note: "By two months of age, and perhaps even at birth, the child is already able to discriminate among, and imitate the facial expressions of, other individuals. This capacity suggests a degree of 'pre-tunedness' to the feelings and behaviors of other individuals that is extraordinary. The child soon distinguishes mother from father, parents from strangers, happy expressions from sad or angry ones. (Indeed, by the end of ten months, the infant's ability to discriminate among different affective expressions already yields distinctive patterns of brain waves.)

"In addition, the child comes to associate various feelings with particular individuals, experiences, and circumstances. There are already the first signs of empathy. The young child will respond sympathetically when he hears the cry of another infant or sees someone in pain: even though the child may not yet appreciate just how the other is feeling, he seems to have a sense that something is not right in the world of another person. A link among familiarity, caring, and altruism has already begun to form" (Gardner, 1983).

This child will (almost always) want to go to school at an early age. Playgroups are particularly satisfying, and their *number one priority* is to be around other children or engage in family gatherings and so forth. Like the linguistic child, they are early talkers, so they always want to be a part of every aspect of your life. They will engage anyone on the street, be it animal or human. If they were a canine, they would be the friendly golden retriever or the pug of the canine world.

When they are around other children, assuming they have passed beyond *parallel play*, they will want to be in charge, telling other children what to do because they like to *talk the talk* and *walk the walk*. In short, it is their way of wanting to interact with the world around them, and for this child to give up control could diminish their interpersonal skills. They should be very empathic, so ask them what they are feeling or thinking and let them talk and share their inner thoughts with you.

These children thrive on any and all social experiences. Again, at six years of age, Johnny Carson took up magic and performed magic shows at birthday parties. Such activities start early, so be flexible and patient with their outgoing personalities.

Brain Changing Note: You can help such students become more aware of their own feelings by taking short breaks during the day (ten to fifteen minutes) to sit quietly and reflect on the daily activities and the impact it had on them.

You should start them early in theater groups to support possible future vocations in theater or drama. In high school, they can join drama clubs and perform in school plays or become captain of the debate team. Like the linguistic intelligence learner, teachers should sit them in the front of the class and may have to call on them more than other students, so that they can talk, explain, and even empathize with other students' opinions, since they desperately need to be interacting.

As with the linguistic child, the internet and social media are made for them. They work best in study groups and love group and family discussions of any length or intensity, which allows them to play the questioning psychologist or lecturing professor. They can be excellent tutors and peer counselors, and a good strategy for learning a lesson is to teach it to someone else.

They will argue with you until the lights are out, but you should not take their arguing or questioning as disrespect; it is only their way of talking and using their interpersonal intelligence to let you know how much they intuitively understand you and life in general.

Brain Changing Note: Google Dr. David Sortino, "Contracts, Adolescence and Family Values."

They could make great lawyers because they can use their perceptive and intuitive intelligence to communicate, interpret, empathize, and convince others. Finally, in the humanistic sector, they can make excellent speech therapists, nurses, public relations workers, teachers, psychologists, and social workers because such professions allow them to work with the public and use their interpersonal intelligence.

Using your knowledge of interpersonal intelligence, describe any unique behaviors your child has exhibited in the following areas:

- Activities include anything associated with problem solving, particularly with their social skills
- Homework/study skills that include story or listening tapes
- Play/activities including theater, playgroups, or clubs
- School interests or activities that include drama class, debate team, running for school office, or peer counseling
- Careers spoken about or demonstrated interests including actor, actress, radio announcer, social worker, psychologist, or teacher

For more ideas, Google "Study Tips Based on Multiple Intelligence (How You Learn)."

INTRAPERSONAL

> In its most primitive form, the intrapersonal intelligence amounts to little more than the capacity to distinguish feelings of pleasure from that of pain and, on the basis of such discrimination, to become more involved in or to withdraw from a situation. At its most advanced level, intrapersonal knowledge allows one to detect and symbolize complex and highly differential sets of feelings. One finds this form of intelligence developed in the novelist such as Proust, who can write introspectively about feelings and life, as in the wise elder who draws his own wealth of inner experiences in order to advise members of his community. (Gardner, 1983)

The quiet, shy, observant infant with the intense look on his face may appear as somewhat timid, but internally he is trying to figure out who he really is and where he fits in his new world. Even at this age, he seems to be aware of his bodily needs and goes to great lengths to convince and even force caregivers to respond to his needs. As he grows older, he will take this skill to a new level and become a person that people can never seem to figure out. His lack of transparency is often his strength as well as his weakness. This child may seem standoffish and mistrustful, but he truly needs and will demand his quiet time alone.

Read to this child in one-to-one situations. Provide picture books and games that he can look through and manipulate. When you buy him toys, he will often play with a toy quietly and alone for hours on end. In some ways, he is like the kinesthetic child and would rather take a toy apart and see how it works because, in his own way, he really is taking *himself apart* to find out who he is and where he fits in. He is not being destructive; it is how his mind tries to figure out the world in which others are always trying to place him. We might assume that because he can be a loner, he must be unhappy, when in reality it is simply his way of reinforcing the intrapersonal intelligence personality.

Brain Changing Note: "A good study skills strategy is to give this student an assignment task and ask them to re-word the question or statement to something that they understand better and feel more comfortable with. Have the student keep a learning log or journal.

"Prominent roles such as chairperson, timekeeper of a group for an assignment requiring group work will allow the student to use their confidence and debating skills. Be aware that intrapersonal learners do not always feel the desire to pursue good grades, as they often feel that their achievements are on a personal level and do not require validation through grades" (Armstrong, 2009).

Teachers can engage this child one-on-one to truly connect, and engagement should encompass things he already knows; then you can move on to areas that are more provocative or challenging. The key is getting this child to feel comfortable expressing his personal opinions, which is why such discussions are important to him. The intrapersonal learner treats conversations and words as if they are *the last words he will ever speak*, so be sure to go with the flow or he will suddenly leave the conversation and simply stop speaking.

Brain Changing Note: "Intrapersonal Intelligence activities may take a while to make a noticeable difference. The key to building Intrapersonal Intelligence is to gain awareness of yourself, which can result in better moods, longer periods of concentration and many other benefits. To become more intelligent in this way, you have to think about what you're thinking—which means stopping yourself every once in a while, and really questioning what's on your mind. Doing so can help you discover when things are not quite right—or when something you're doing is working really well for you" (Armstrong, 2009).

Moreover, he does not feel uncomfortable pursuing eccentric ideas because his strong intuitive sense allows him to see the idea from deeper angles or levels. On the other hand, he could be a reflective learner who may need more time to process information before he blurts out the answer.

Brain Changing Note: "Many people think intuition is just a form of guessing. Actually, it is much more. Some researchers say it is 'the highest form of Intelligence.' Is it? We often call it our 'gut feel.' Well, our gut doesn't do any thinking except perhaps telling us we are hungry. 'Gut feel' is intuition. Often, we are ready to make a decision, but feel uncomfortable about it for some reason. That could be intuition, giving us a subtle warning" (Dohmen, 2018).

Also, he will rarely raise his hand in a class discussion, regardless of the fact that he knows the answer. Therefore, with such children, teachers need to gently probe for answers; otherwise, he will sit quietly in the back of the room never uttering a word.

Such children are highly introspective and intuitive, so the more you probe, the more information will flow from their quiet personalities.

In middle and high school, they could work as volunteers in the library or sound technician with school plays, but they always prefer to stay on the outside looking in.

In college, they could study anything that stimulates their introspective needs, such as philosophy, psychology, writing, or theology. They are the Henry David Thoreaus of the world who can be happy living alone dissecting nature at Walden Pond, a horticulturalist tending to a garden, a writer, or a scientist who spends hours alone in the laboratory developing some great theory or cure for humanity.

Using your knowledge of intrapersonal intelligence, describe any unique behaviors your child has exhibited in the following areas:

- Activities including anything associated with problem-solving skills, self-direction, or testing yourself on a new skill
- Homework/study skills that include story or listening tapes or school schedules

- Play/activities including theater, playgroups, or chess clubs
- School interests or activities that support journal or creative writing
- Careers spoken about or demonstrated interests including writer, accountant, or medical researcher

For more ideas, Google "Study Tips Based on Multiple Intelligence (How You Learn)."

NATURALIST

Some primary examples of notable people having naturalistic intelligence are John Muir, Rachel Carson, Charles Darwin, John James Audubon, Jacques Cousteau, David Suzuki, Jane Goodall, Steve Irwin, Neil deGrasse Tyson, as well as a host of famous explorers like Lewis and Clark.

At the earliest age, place this infant into a backpack and hike, letting all their senses experience the sights and sounds of nature.

With the advent of toddlerhood, help them build gardens, plant flowers and vegetables, and make field trips to parks and nature preserves a weekly experience.

Zoobooks, *Natural Geographic*, or any magazines or books associated with nature should fill his room, and animal photos should be allowed to be plastered on his walls.

Early childhood creates question-and-answer time, so use this time for dialogue, relating to the nurturing of a flower, while their probing curiosity about nature is still food for their minds. As should be the case with all children, you should show them films and read biographies of naturalists like Thoreau, Beatrix Potter, Rachel Carson, and John Muir. In school, they need to touch, feel, and use their senses with assignments to create answers as to why the sky is actually blue.

Brain Changing Note: "Our ability to recognize faces may be closely allied to our naturalist intelligence" (Gardner, 1983).

These individuals are often confused with the kinesthetic learner because they gravitate to the outside at an early age, experiencing the world of nature with such activities as climbing trees or digging their hands in the pulse of earth's soil and mud. This could be the child who will be collecting rocks, sticks, and insects at a very early age. They could be the child tracking mud into the house because they have been outside in the garden looking for worms or trying to grow a vegetable from seed. In short, gardening and nature walks should start early and be a frequent part of their day.

They are good at seeing nature's subtle organizations and should keep a journal, not only of words but also for drawings of nature to express their thoughts and feelings for self-reflections. At ten years of age, Piaget's documentation of a sparrow at a Geneva park led him on a scientific journey to becoming one of the world's foremost cognitive psychologists.

Brain Changing Note: "Many educators know of young students who know all there is to know about dinosaurs, butterflies, fish, rocks, etc. They have a deep interest in and fascination with something in nature and are driven to investigate and become an 'expert' in a particular natural subject. These are the students who exhibit naturalist intelligence" (Karen, 1999).

These children can make graphs to systemize knowledge and show relationships between living and nonliving things. Most importantly, children who demonstrate a naturalist intelligence have been shown to actually intuit the needs of animals and plants they love.

Moreover, they could be the leaders in school science projects, so let them take the lead in the classroom, regardless of how complex or innocent the process may become.

In elementary school, they may want to start a classroom flower or vegetable garden on the school grounds. In the classroom, teachers should put them in charge of watering plants and caring for the aquarium and any pets that may inhabit the classroom.

Again, parents need to take them to nature farms, science museums, and animal rescue centers and sign them up as volunteers at the town's annual cleanup days. At home, they need pets like gerbils and rabbits to express their naturalist intelligence.

Brain Changing Note: "Your student or child may be "nature smart" if he or she consistently displays some of the following behaviors:

1. Notices patterns and rhythms from their surroundings easily—observing likes, differences, similarities, or anomalies
2. Can pinpoint things in their surroundings or environments others often miss

3. Has a sharp memory for details, often observing and easily remembering things from his/her environment and surroundings
4. Has keen senses (sight, hearing, sense of touch and smell, and may even have a well-developed "sixth sense")
5. Likes animals and likes to know and remember things about them
6. Really appreciates being outside and doing things like gardening, camping, hiking or climbing, exploring, and even just like sitting quietly and noticing the subtle differences in the world of nature
7. Makes astute observations about natural changes and emerging patterns, natural phenomena, human populations, and the existing or possible connection or interconnections
8. Loves books, shows, or videos about nature or natural phenomena, or animals
9. Creates, keeps or has collections, scrapbooks, logs, or journals about natural objects—these may include written observations, drawings, pictures and photographs or specimens
10. Shows a heightened awareness and/or concern, even empathy, for the environment and/or for endangered species
11. Easily learns characteristics, names, categorizations, and data about objects or species found in the natural world
12. Often displays a sense of wonder, awe, or surprise for/or about the natural world or natural phenomena" (Wilson, 2018a).

In high school, they can become involved with 4-H, agriculture, botany, biology clubs, or as chief organizer of the annual town cleanup. In college, their interests are associated with the sciences, such as agriculture, environmental studies, and summer jobs with the state or national park service.

Careers follow their college interests into areas such as environmental law, national park service, animal rescue centers, and of course, veterinary medicine.

Brain Changing Note: "When you connect a new idea or pattern of life in the natural world, and how humans are part of this ecology, then understanding is immense" (Shearer, 2004b).

Finally, they can take a year off from school and backpack to far-off places, keeping a journal or taking photos for future publications. In so many ways, they could become a John Muir mapping the Yosemite backwoods or a Rachel Carlson (author of *Silent Spring*) forecasting the importance of protecting the environment.

Using your knowledge of naturalist intelligence, describe any unique behaviors or interests your child has exhibited in the following areas:

- Activities including anything associated with understanding animals or nature
- Homework/study skills that include sensory perception, nature journals, or nature clubs
- Play/activities including starting a garden or taking nature hikes
- Careers spoken about or demonstrated interests such as naturalist, forester, or landscape designer
- School interests or activities such as horticulture, gardening, or early science

For more ideas, Google "Study Tips Based on Multiple Intelligence (How You Learn)."

Brain Changing Note: See the appendix for information on MIDAS (Multiple Intelligence Developmental Assessment Scales).

Chapter Three

Psychosocial Development

*Tapping into Your Child's Social Intelligence
—Dr. Erik Erikson (1902–1994)*

A major contributor to the brain changer concept is Erik Erikson and his psychosocial theory. Erikson was a stage theorist who modified Freud's psychosexual theory to create eight stages of psychosocial development (trust vs. mistrust, autonomy vs. shame/doubt, initiative vs. guilt, industry vs. inferiority, identity vs. role confusion, intimacy vs. isolation, generativity vs. stagnation, and integrity vs. despair). Google Freud's psychosexual theory for additional information.

Erikson's eight stages define two opposing ideas that individuals need to resolve successfully to become a so-called positive contributor to society. In fact, an inability to accomplish this responsibility can lead to a lack of accomplishment in other areas of human development.

Brain Changing Note: "You see a child play, and it is so close to seeing an artist paint, for in play a child says things without uttering a word. You can see how he solves his problems. You can also see what's wrong. Young children, especially, have enormous creativity, and whatever's in them rises to the surface in free play" (Brainy Quotes, 2019).

Erikson's' first stage, *trust vs. mistrust* (ages 0 to 18 months), describes why trust is crucial to your child's learning brain and why this stage should be considered the most important foundation for all other stages to follow since a lack of trust could weaken all the other stages that follow.

This stage is extenuated by the need for the infant to develop a deep sense of trust with his caregivers. For example, breastfeeding is critically important to the infant's brain because when the infant receives nurturance and predictability from his caregiver's breastfeeding, this interaction stimulates *bonding*, which connects with the brain's hippocampus. Brain scientists believe that the hippocampus serves as a future link to higher-order thinking. Equally important, the hippocampus is said to be the only area of the brain that allows neurons to regenerate, which is obviously advantageous for the infant's developing young brain.

Brain Changing Note: "Breast milk contains all the nutrients that an infant requires in the first 6 months of life, including fat, carbohydrates, proteins, vitamins, minerals and water. It is easily digested and efficiently used. Breast milk also contains bioactive factors that augment the infant's immature immune system, providing protection against infection, and other factors that help digestion and absorption of nutrients" (World Health Organization, 2009).

Moreover, infants who develop a *sense of trust* experience a sense of optimism, confidence, and general well-being. However, when the infant experiences a sense of *mistrust* as a result of his basic biological needs not being met (food, physical touch, emotional love, etc.), a sense of *mistrust* is established in the infant's brain. His or her interpretation of the world can become one of unpredictability and lack of security. Consequently, a lack of confidence can follow.

Brain Changing Note: "The process of bonding with a new baby is natural for most mothers. Left alone, new mothers will hold their baby next to their bodies, rock them gently, strive for eye contact, sing or talk to the baby and begin to nurse. Often within just hours of birth, mothers report feelings of overwhelming love and attachment for their new baby.

"A normal, full-term baby is also programmed to initiate and enter into a bonding relationship. Crying and making other noises, smiling, searching for the breast, and seeking eye contact give cues for a caring adult to respond.

"When a caregiver consistently responds to an infant's needs, a trusting relationship and lifelong attachment develops. This sets the stage for the growing child to enter healthy relationships with other people throughout life and to appropriately experience and express a full range of emotions" (Steinfeld, 2018).

Brain Changing Note: "Reactive attachment disorder (RAD) is a condition found in children who may have received grossly negligent care and do not form a healthy emotional attachment with their primary caregivers—usually their mothers—before age 5. Attachment develops when a child is repeatedly soothed, comforted, and cared for, and when the caregiver consistently meets the child's needs.

"It is through attachment with a loving and protective caregiver that a young child learns to love and trust others, to become aware of others' feelings and needs, to regulate his or her emotions, and to develop healthy relationships and a positive self-image. The absence of emotional warmth during the first few years of life can negatively affect a child's entire future" (WebMD, 2018).

Erikson's second stage, *autonomy vs. doubt and shame* (ages 1 to 3), characterizes children whose major interest is the exploration of their world. This is a time of self-esteem development associated with degrees of autonomy or the ability to expand the territory caregivers can safely allow. In addition, they are also beginning to establish a sense of *autonomy or preference* for toys and clothing, as well as for food needs. It is also a period of the *terrible twos*, when stubbornness, defiance, and tantrums appear.

The dilemma for caregivers is how to allow the child at this stage of development the space to establish independence without forcing greater controls over his need to be autonomous. Conversely, parents who are overly controlling or deny this child the opportunity to act on his needs for autonomy can create a sense of doubt in the child's abilities and a sense of shame can ensue, affecting our next stage of development.

Brain Changing Note: The "Strange Situation" was designed to present children with an unusual, but not overwhelmingly frightening, experience (Ainsworth, Blehar, Waters, & Wall, 1978). When a child undergoes the "Strange Situation," researchers are interested in two things: how much the child explores the room on his own, and how the child responds to the return of his mother.

To test a child's *attachment style*, researchers place a child (12 to 18 months) and her mother alone in an experimental room. The room has toys or other interesting things, and the mother lets the child explore the room on her own. After the child has had time to explore, a stranger enters the room and talks with the mother. Then the stranger shifts attention to the child. As the stranger approaches the child, the mother sneaks away. After several minutes, the mother returns. She comforts her child and then leaves again. The stranger leaves as well. A few minutes later, the stranger returns and interacts with the child. Finally, the mother returns and greets her child.

Typically, a child's response to the "Strange Situation" follows one of four patterns.

Securely attached children: free exploration and happiness upon the mother's return. The securely attached child explores the room freely when his mother is present. He may be distressed when his mother leaves, and he explores less when she is absent. But he is happy when she returns. If he cries, he approaches his mother and holds her tightly. He is comforted by being held, and once comforted he is soon ready to resume his independent exploration of the world. His mother is responsive to his needs. As a result, he knows he can depend on her when he is under stress (Ainsworth, Blehar, Waters, & Wall, 1978).

Avoidant-insecure children: little exploration and little emotional response to the mother. The avoidant-insecure child doesn't explore much, and she doesn't show much emotion when her mother leaves. She shows no preference for her mother over a complete stranger. When her mother returns, she tends to avoid or ignore her (Ainsworth, Blehar, Waters, & Wall, 1978).

Resistant-insecure (also called "anxious" or "ambivalent") children: little exploration, great separation anxiety, and an ambivalent response to the mother upon her return. Like the avoidant child, the resistant-insecure child doesn't explore much on his own. But unlike the avoidant child, the resistant child is wary of strangers and is very distressed when his mother leaves. When the mother returns, the resistant child is ambivalent. Although he wants to reestablish close proximity to his mother, he is also resentful—even angry—at his mother for leaving him in the first place. As a result, the resistant child may reject his mother's attempts at contact (Ainsworth, Blehar, Waters, & Wall, 1978).

Disorganized-insecure children: little exploration and a confused response to the mother. The disorganized child may exhibit a mix of avoidant and resistant behaviors. But the main theme is one of confusion and anxiety (Main & Solomon, 1986). Disorganized-insecure children are at risk for a variety of behavioral and developmental problems (Dewar, 2018).

Initiative vs. guilt (ages 3 to 4) ushers in the preschool stage and represents the child who feels secure *initiating activities* and even control over social interactions with play activities. His main challenge is how to get his needs met or goals achieved, while still feeling confident interacting within the playgroup or one to one with other siblings? His strong need to copy adults can conflict with taking the initiative in play, which can affect this child's sense of *ambition and confidence*. Additionally, those children who are unsuccessful in finding a sense of purpose at this stage due to overly controlling caregivers are often blocked. They will often lack initiative and carry a *sense of guilt*.

Brain Changing Note: "The regulation of behavior is a major issue in early childhood development, with important implications for children's adaptive and maladaptive developmental outcomes. Emerging research suggests that the degree of successful self-regulation depends upon the efficiency of the child's attentional system and that the ability to focus and sustain attention supports emotional self-regulation throughout the lifespan.

"The neural networks that underlie the development of attention are beginning to be charted. Studies have shown that the executive attention network undergoes considerable development between the ages of 2 and 7. To support this development, research scholars have suggested the need to develop curriculum to promote focused and sustained attention in preschool programs" (Lloyd, 2018).

Brain Changing Note: "Exploring the inside and outside world—with supervision, of course—is important for toddlers' emotional, social, and physical development. They learn more about the world and how it works. It's one thing to see an orange, but it's another to hold it in your hand, feel it's cool, smooth surface, smell its fragrance, maybe even taste it. That development is all the better if you ask questions: What color is it? Is it big or little? Exploring also gives toddlers a chance to work on important motor skills.

"Whether it's kicking a ball or climbing stairs, they can persist until they get it right. Doing so not only adds skills, it boosts their sense of confidence and competence. In other words, they begin to think: 'I can do it!' Letting kids explore is one way to see that toddlers get enough daily physical activity. Exploring fits well in that free-play category below. For kids 12- to 36-months-old, current guidelines from the National Association for Sports & Physical Education (NAPE) recommend at least 30 minutes of structured physical activity (adult-led), and at least 60 minutes of unstructured physical activity (free play)" (Gavin, 2015).

Brain Changing Note: "Play has been a controversial term in the Montessori classroom since Dr. Montessori claimed the word "work" as both a noun and a verb to describe her children's activities. However, many activities that are termed 'work' in the Montessori classroom might be called 'play' in a traditional preschool. In addition, evidence of playful learning can be seen throughout the Montessori philosophy. Current research demonstrates that play is beneficial for children in a variety of developmental areas, and different types of play are expected and associated with different stages" (O'Connor, 2015).

Brain Changing Note: "The Montessori philosophy is dedicated to meeting all of the developmental needs of the 'whole child' so that he or she may grow into an intellectually curious, compassionate, peaceful, and productive member of society. Montessori teachers must consider play as a developmental area, and observe and guide the children's movements in the classroom to support their growth. This action research aims to introduce materials and activities that could be termed 'play' or contain play-like qualities into the classroom with the same amount of preparation, analysis, and sequencing as all of the other Montessori materials, with an informed perspective based on knowledge and observation" (O'Connor, 2015).

Our fourth stage, *industry vs. inferiority*, is one of the most important psychosocial stages because it serves as a *bridge* to our next stage. At this stage, children constantly compare and contrast themselves with the peer group, an activity that is considered their foremost concern at this stage. They are highly capable of accomplishing new skills and knowledge, hence the sense of being *industrious*. However, unless they are able to fulfill a sense of accomplishment, feelings of inadequacy and inferiority can develop in peers and family relationships. In short, the inability to establish a sense of industry can have major ramifications on the upcoming stages.

Brain Changing Note: Google Dr. David Sortino, "Throw Like a Girl?"

Moreover, if a child leaves this stage with a *sense of inferiority* (an inferiority complex), the stage of adolescence could be ten times more difficult! However, with industry can come success in school, sports, academics, and self-esteem. Nevertheless, an inability to create a sense of industry creates a sense of inferiority and fear of failure.

Brain Changing Note: "Perhaps the best way to visualize how the industry versus inferiority stage might impact a child is to look at an example. Imagine two children in the same fourth grade class. Olivia finds science lessons difficult, but her parents are willing to help her each night with her homework. She also asks the teacher for help and starts to receive encouragement and praise for her efforts. Jack also struggles with science, but his parents are uninterested in assisting him with his nightly homework. He feels bad about the poor grades he receives on his science assignments but is not sure what to do about the situation. His teacher is critical of his work but does not offer any extra assistance or advice. Eventually, Jack just gives up, and his grades become even worse.

"While both children struggled with this aspect of school, Olivia received the support and encouragement she needed to overcome these difficulties and still build a sense of mastery. Jack, however, lacked the social and emotional encouragement he needed. In this area, Olivia will likely develop a sense of industry whereas Jack will be left with feelings of inferiority" (Cherry, 2018).

Brain Changing Note: Google Dr. David Sortino, "Why Student's Underachieve."

A student's success in the fifth stage, *identity vs. role confusion* (adolescence, ages 12 to 18), is often determined by the previous four stages of psychosocial development. That is, if the earlier stages are unresolved, problems can develop with social development or how the adolescent comes to terms with *finding one's true identity*, such as fitting into the norms of their peer group. Also, a key area will be *moral judgment* and how he is able to balance right and wrong. Major questions about who I am or what can I do with my life are paramount with the adolescent psyche.

Brain Changing Note: Google Dr. David Sortino, "Absentee Fathers and Juvenile Justice."

In addition, today's bombardment from social media is placing greater pressure on the *who I am* question that other generations never had to deal with. Nonetheless, adolescents who succeed during this trying and challenging period are those who develop a strong identity and remain strong in their beliefs and values, regardless of influences from the peer group.

Unfortunately, those adolescents who do not make a conscious effort for a successful identity could become ambivalent about their role in society, resulting in a sense of *role confusion*.

Brain Changing Note: "Juveniles constitute 1,200 of the 1.5 million people housed in federal and state prisons in this country, and nearly 200,000 youth enter the adult criminal-justice system each year, most for non-violent crimes. On any given day, 10,000 juveniles are housed in adult prisons and jails. These children lose more than their freedom when they enter adult prisons; they lose out on the educational and psychological benefits offered by juvenile-detention facilities. Worse, they are much more likely to suffer sexual abuse and violence at the hands of other inmates and prison staff.

The National Prison Rape Elimination Commission described their fate in blunt terms in a 2009 report: 'More than any other group of incarcerated persons, youth incarcerated with adults are probably at the highest risk of sexual abuse'" (Lahey, 2016).

The sixth stage, *intimacy vs. isolation* (ages 18–35), ushers in young adulthood and is dominated by a desire for companionship and mature love. During this stage, the need for intimacy and secure relationships is paramount, and unless the sense of intimacy is well grounded, such as knowing oneself or needs, this stage can result in isolation.

For example, the high divorce rate in our society could be caused by an inability to establish intimate, secure relationships due to weaknesses in our previous stages. In addition, many young adults at this stage have had to put off marriage due to lack of education and job skills and economic difficulties.

Brains Changing Note: "I can't even imagine paying for a wedding right now," 26-year-old Kaitlyn Schaefer explains. The grad student splits her time between teaching special education kids and running to class, all the while accumulating tens of thousands of dollars in student debt. Oh, did I mention she just celebrated her 10th anniversary with her boyfriend? But no, marriage isn't on the table at the moment.

"For many young people across the country, putting off marriage—or even settling down with a partner long term—has become the norm. The average age for first marriage is 27 for women and 29 for men; in urban areas such as New York and Washington, those averages are higher. It seems that everyone has a different answer for why: Blame it on the economy. Or dating apps. Or women's ability to delay child bearing" (Barkho, 2016).

Middle-aged adults (ages 35 to 55) enter our seventh stage, *generativity vs. self-absorption*. During this period, individuals are involved with stability, raising a family, making a contribution to society, such as assuming greater responsibilities for the good of mankind. In addition, there are major life changes during this stage, such as children leaving the home for school, career, and marriage. An inability to establish or maintain generativity can result in stagnation or self-absorption, and such an adult will never establish relationships with others or find a place in society.

Brain Changing Note: "More women in the U.S. are childless than at any other time since the government began keeping track, a new survey found. Nearly half of women between the ages of 15 and 44 did not have kids in 2014, up from 46.5% in 2012 to 47.6% in 2014, according to new data from the U.S. Census Bureau's Current Population Survey. The figure is the highest percentage since the Census Bureau started measuring it in 1976. Among women between 25 and 29, 49.6% were childless in 2014, also an all-time high. In the group between 30 and 34, 28.9% were childless, up from 28.2% in 2012 but below an all-time high of 29.7% in 2010. As of 2013, the general fertility rate in the U.S., as measured by the number of babies' women gave birth to, between 15 and 44, had fallen for six straight years and sat at 1.86, according to the *New York Times*. Maintaining a stable U.S. population would require a fertility rate of 2.1" (Luckerson, 2015).

The late adult stage (ages 55 and older) is called *integrity vs. despair* and accounts for individuals who feel fulfilled by their accomplishments and life experiences and exhibit a deep sense of integrity. They have a sense of contentment and fulfillment to support their sense of integrity through positive family, community, and career interaction. Conversely, those who have failed to develop this sense of fulfillment experience a sense of despair and a perception that their lives have been a failure. The end result is that they face the end of their lives with a sense of bitterness, desperation, and despair, or what some would describe as the "Ebenezer Scrooge syndrome."

Brain Changing Note: Google Dr. David Sortino, "Volunteering in School Is Good for Your Brain."

Brain Changing Note: "Calling All Grandparents: Senior Volunteers Transform Schools. They are reliable and passionate, and they bring learning and love to urban classrooms. They are Experience Corps volunteers—retirees recruited and trained to tutor students and assist teachers. Volunteers and educators alike have nothing but praise for the program" (Education World, 2018).

Chapter Four

Moral Development

The Development of the Moral Child
—Dr. Lawrence Kohlberg (1927–1987)

> If brief periods of classroom discussion can have a substantial effect on moral development, a pervasive influence upon moral development should have much deeper effects. Such a concern would pervade the curriculum areas of social studies, law education, philosophy and sex education, rather than representing new curriculum areas. More deeply, it would affect the social atmosphere and justice structure of the school. (Reimer, Pritchard Paolitto, & Hersh, 1999)

My first teaching experience occurred at a day treatment school for youth with special needs and challenges. In retrospect, this position was my first step toward personally and professionally understanding how *moral development theory* could help me be a more effective teacher.

Along with my seriously emotionally disturbed (SED) program was the "physically handicapped program," composed of ten pregnant teens ages thirteen to nineteen; the "trainable mentally retarded" (TMR) program, ages eight to nineteen; and the autistic program, ages ten to twenty-one.

The pregnant teens were facing serious difficulties: how to deal with the birth of a child when they were still so confused about their own lives. Coupled with the teens' personal situations were problems that surfaced between the pregnant teens program and a twelve-year-old boy in my SED program named Richard.

Richard's hatred of the pregnant teens was linked to how extremely he had suffered under the physical and emotional abuse of his deceased alcoholic mother. Although he received counseling from a kindly female psychologist and our wonderful female staff, his displaced anger toward the teens was holding him back from ever returning to public school. "They are whores!" he would scream. "They are ruining the reputation of our school!"

I knew that Richard loved horses, and after much research on my part I was able to find a horse farm near our school that was run by a young childless couple. I called the farm, and after much hesitation from the owner regarding safety and insurance, he cautiously agreed to have Richard work two afternoons a week cleaning stalls, feeding the horses in exchange for cookies and milk.

One afternoon, after about a month at the farm, Richard appeared at school, breathless and excited, as he showed me knitted gloves that he held close to his body. "Susan knitted me a pair of gloves! It's the best gift I ever got!" he explained excitedly. "Really, the best gift ever!"

About a week later, I noticed Richard on our school patio showing his knitted gloves to several of the pregnant teens that who were knitting booties for their expected babies. The gift of the knitted gloves had made such an impression on Richard that he asked the teens to teach him how to knit. Richard's knitting lessons soon became a regular activity with the teens he had once despised.

One afternoon, when I was making my rounds around the school, I came into the pregnant teens classroom and found Richard sitting on a chair with three of the young women, all knitting. Quietly, I asked Richard what he was knitting, and he replied, "I am knitting a uterus so the girls can pass a baby doll through it so they can see how a baby is born."

An abused boy hates all females. A teacher needs to find a connection for the boy to trust women again. A pair of knitted gloves fosters a positive relationship between him and a group of people he once despised. Richard, through the work of his teachers and the care of a young couple who took him in, was able to move in just a matter of weeks from Kohlberg's Stage 2 (self-centered) to Stage 3 (more considerate to the feelings and needs of others).

The rest of this chapter gives further understanding of the stages of moral development. As you learn about moral development theory, try to apply the theory to personal experiences with your own children or students. With a little understanding of moral development theory, you'll be able to stimulate the process of moral growth for your students and children.

THE STAGES OF MORAL DEVELOPMENT

Just as children think in cognitive stages, so do they think in moral stages. Based on his twenty-year longitudinal study and cross-cultural research, Harvard psychologist Lawrence Kohlberg described five stages of moral reasoning. Later research by William Damon and Robert Selman added a stage that describes children's moral reasoning during the preschool period. Each moral stage has a different idea of what's right and a different idea of the reason why a person should be good. Each stage of moral development brings a person a step closer to a fully developed morality of respect for self, others, and society.

The ages below indicate when a stage typically first appears in an individual of normal intelligence growing up in a supportive moral environment. It is common for children to show stage mix, with one stage being dominant. Under stress, a person may regress to lower stages.

Stage 0: Egocentric Reasoning; "My Way or the Cry Way" (Preschool Years)

At Stage 0 of moral reasoning, kids think that what's right is to get what they want. While two-year-olds say, "I want it!" Four-year-olds think, "I want it and it's not fair if I don't get it!" That may not seem like developmental progress, but it is—in the sense that they are now using the language of fairness and seeing things from a moral viewpoint. It's a very egocentric viewpoint, to be sure, but it's part of the gradual growth of learning to think about questions of fairness and unfairness, right and wrong.

Helping Children Move from Stage 0 to Stage 1 Moral Reasoning

From their "my way or the cry way" perspective, Stage 0 thinkers believe the world *should* be the kind of place where they get what they want when they want it. Progress beyond this way of thinking requires finding out they *can't* have everything they want—that there are rules they have to obey and consequences when they don't. That means parents and teachers have to be very clear about their behavioral expectations and enforce them consistently.

Stage 0: Egocentric Reasoning; "My Way or the Cry Way" (preschool years; around 4)	What's Right:	I should get my own way.
	Reason to Be Good:	To get rewards and avoid punishments.
Stage 1: "Stay out of Trouble" (around kindergarten age)	What's Right:	I should do what I'm told.
	Reason to Be Good:	To stay out of trouble.
Stage 2: Tit-for-Tat Fairness; "Look out for Yourself" (early elementary grades)	What's Right:	I should look out for myself but also do for those who do for me.
	Reason to Be Good:	Self-interest: What's in it for me?
Stage 3: Interpersonal Conformity; "What Will Others Think of Me?" (middle to upper elementary grades; early to midteens)	What's Right:	I should be a nice person and live up to the expectations of people I know and care about.
	Reason to Be Good:	So others will think well of me (social approval) and I can think well of myself (self-esteem).
Stage 4: Responsibility to Society; "I Should Be a Responsible Person and Good Citizen" (high school years/late teens/college)	What's Right:	I should fulfill my responsibilities to the social or value system I feel part of (church, my country, etc.).
	Reason to Be Good:	To keep society from falling apart and to maintain my self-respect as somebody who meets my obligations.
Stage 5: Respect the Rights of Every Person (late teens, early adulthood and later)	What's Right:	I should show the greatest possible respect for the rights and dignity of every individual person and should support a system that protects human rights.

In dealing with Stage 0 kids, it helps to appeal to their self-interest while simultaneously requiring compliance with adult expectations.

For example, suppose your four-year-old starts to protest and cry when you tell him it's time to go home from the playground. You could say calmly but firmly, "Look, if you make a big fuss when I say it's time to go home, will I want to bring you to the playground the next time you ask?" You're coming down to your child's developmental level by appealing to his self-interest, but doing so in a way that makes it clear you expect respect for your authority and obedience.

Stage 1: "Stay Out of Trouble" (Age 5 and Up)

At Stage 1, which often emerges around age five, kids think it's right to obey their parents and teachers. That's further progress; they now accept the reality that adults are in charge and there's a social order that kids have to fit into. But their best reason for following adults' rules is "I'll get punished if I don't." Unfortunately, this kind of thinking does not guarantee rule following, because when the authority figure is out of sight, the rule is often out of mind.

The limitations of this punishment-focused thinking are evident from a conversation with a ten-year-old boy named Hank who had been caught several times stealing from other kids' lockers in school. When the school psychologist asked Hank if he thought stealing was right or wrong, Hank answered without hesitating, "Wrong." When the psychologist asked him why it was wrong, Hank said, "Because the principal might catch you, and you'd be in big trouble." Asked if he could think of another reason why stealing was wrong, Hank said, "Because the cops might catch you, and you'd have to go to jail." Asked again if he could think of another reason why you shouldn't steal, Hank said, "Because if your old man found out, you'd get a whippin' when you got home."

In all three of Hank's explanations, he took only one point of view, that of *authority figures with the power to punish*. Whose point of view did he fail to consider? That of the victims of his thefts.

Hank was still stuck in Stage 1 thinking at an age when most children have progressed at least to a Stage 2 sense of fairness ("If you steal from other people, it will be fair for them to do the same to you"). The research of Kohlberg and others finds that all kids develop through the same moral stages in the same order, but they do so at different rates. Individual differences in rates of moral development can be attributed to the moral environment.

If the moral environment does not provide children with enough opportunities to take the perspective of others—to enter into their thinking and feelings—then developmental progress is slowed, and an immature stage of reasoning might remain dominant for a long time.

Hank's description of what his father might do if he found out he'd stolen something suggests that his moral training at home was long on "whippin's" and short on the sort of moral reasoning that could have helped Hank develop beyond Stage's 1's narrow focus on avoiding punishment as the reason to follow rules.

Helping Children Move from Stage 1 to Stage 2 Moral Reasoning

When children are at Stage 1, adults need to take the reins and provide the control and boundaries due to the child's dependence on authority and weak inner controls. However, my-way-or-the-highway discipline that never explains the reasons behind rules will only reinforce Stage 1's primitive obey-to-avoid-punishment orientation.

In order to promote development to Stage 2, adults must help Stage 1 children understand the moral logic behind rules: they enable us to live together and get along. We also need to teach Stage 1 kids the *reciprocal fairness* of Stage 2 moral reasoning: "I did something for you, so it's only fair for you to do something for me."

For example, six-year-old Michael asked his father to read him a story, and he did. But later, when Michael's father asked him to help clean up the kitchen, Michael said he didn't want to. "Hey," his father said, "remember how I read you a story when you asked me to? Now I'm asking you to do something for me. Fair enough?" Michael complied. This kind of reasoning helps kids learn to consider two perspectives—theirs and yours—at the same time. Any time you discuss and solve problems in a way you both consider fair, you're helping children expand their perspective to include two points of view.

Progress beyond Stage 1 can also be fostered by exposing children to positive role models through developmentally appropriate books and movies with prosocial themes. Books and films can also teach children how *not* to act. For example, Joy Berry's *Help Me Be Good* picture book series (for four- to seven-year-olds) uses engaging cartoon art to explain what's wrong with specific bad habits (being bossy, being selfish, being mean, etc.), how such behaviors negatively affect family members and friends, and how to replace those bad habits with good ones.

Stage 2: Tit-for-Tat Fairness; "Look out for Yourself" (Age 7 and Up)

At Stage 2, which typically emerges in the early elementary school years, kids think there's more to morality than just following grown-ups' rules. They believe—and usually assert!—that kids have rights, just like adults, and that everyone should be able to do what they think is right. Feeling like moral equals, they now see social interactions as a process of negotiating for what they want ("You get to go to bed at 10:00 p.m., so why not me?").

The rule of reciprocity becomes central in kids' thinking. They believe that if they're nice to parents, parents should be nice to them ("You scratch my back, and I'll scratch yours"). They view tit-for-tat fairness as applying to peers as well as parents; what's right is to return favor for favor and blow for blow ("an eye for an eye").

Because they've lost much of their fear of adults, kids at this stage may sometimes do things behind your back if they think they can get away with it. And some may regress to lying, cheating, fighting, name-calling, and payback in response to not getting their own way unless they believe such actions are wrong because of the moral values you've been able to instill. In these ways, Stage 2 kids can be more challenging to parent and less sensitive to others than they were at Stage 1—requiring greater efforts on your part to hold them accountable to the family values.

Brain Changing Note: "The 'fairness approach' provides a new challenge by introducing the *language* of fairness into the picture. By using the word 'fair,' you put your concern for fairness up front. Basically, the fairness approach says to a child, 'I'm willing to treat you fairly. But I insist on fairness in return'" (Lickona, 1983). Dr. Thomas Lickona is a developmental psychologist and professor of education emeritus at the State University of New York at Cortland, where he directs the Center for the Fourth and Fifth Rs (Respect and Responsibility). He is a past president of the Association for Moral Education.

Helping Children Move from Stage 2 to Stage 3 Moral Reasoning

Given the way Stage 2 kids see the world, we can expect that they will sometimes talk back and complain about our rules and limits, but as parents we should always insist on respect ("Our family does not talk to each other that way").

We should give immediate, clear, and firm feedback whenever kids cross the line into disrespect ("Can you say that more respectfully?," "Do you need to go to your room and calm down, and we'll talk about this later?").

To encourage Stage 3 thinking, parents should foster love and support of family values in a way that goes beyond tit-for-tat fairness. For instance, "When I help you with your homework, it's not because I expect something in return but because I love you and want to support you!"

Brain Changing Note: "A positive parenting trend is that middle-class parents these days spend a lot more time with their offspring than they used to. One analysis of 11 rich countries estimates that the average mother spent 54 minutes a day caring for children in 1965 but 104 minutes in 2012. Men do less than women, but far more than men in the past: their child-caring time has jumped from 16 minutes a day to 59" (Economist, 2017).

To reinforce family values, close the week with a family meeting where you express appreciation for what someone in the family did that week and put heads together to plan how to make the coming week as cooperative and peaceful as possible. This taps into the positive power of the group, which will help to foster a Stage 3 desire to enjoy a positive identity within the family.

Help kids extend relationships beyond the family, but always be sure to let them know that you will never tolerate their being mistreated or disrespected by others, especially by the peer group. At Stage 2, the peer group can become especially cruel and can disrupt transitioning to Stage 3 thinking. However, if you put the time and energy into developing a good relationship with your child, you will see the positive results during adolescence when they begin to feel safe to speak to you about their personal problems, particularly about friends.

Remember, one of the reasons they talk on their cell phones so much is that they are trying to *define themselves*. The best way to do that—much better than living in the virtual world of fickle and unpredictable "likes"—is through real-life relationships with true friends and family members who love them.

A trusting relationship with loving parents and good friends will go a long way toward establishing a secure identity grounded in good values.

The surest way to raise kids to Stage 3 thinking and behavior is to get them to volunteer in senior citizen homes, Humane Society animal shelters, preschools, and the like. Volunteering moves them out of the self-centered box of Stage 2 thinking and enables them to experience a wider world. That engages their higher brain centers and stimulates the brain development that underlies the development of higher moral reasoning.

Brain Changing Note: "When you're overwhelmed with your responsibilities, it's easy to toggle into automatic pilot with your kids. But if your mind is elsewhere during the precious moments you've worked hard to preserve, you have lost your kids' childhood just as surely as if you hadn't spent the time with them at all. Instead, try to stay in the moment with a 'parenting meditation,' in which you focus on seeing your kids, hearing them, understanding them, and really being amazed by what you've created—living, breathing miracles of nature who are soaking up knowledge like sponges and growing like weeds" (Rotbart, 2012).

Stage 3: Interpersonal Conformity: "What Will Others Think of Me?" (10 and Up)

At Stage 3 moral reasoning, children want to "fit in," to live up to the expectations of others—so that others will think well of them and they can think well of themselves.

At Stage 3, the approval of peers becomes more important than ever. That becomes a problem if friends exert peer pressure to engage in unhealthy or antisocial behaviors such as sex, drugs, drinking, pornography, or lawbreaking. More than ever, parents need to be vigilant about where children are, what they're doing, who they're hanging out with, and so on. Research shows that teens do better in school and avoid harmful behavior if their parents exercise age-appropriate supervision of their activities.

Brain Changing Note: Google Dr. David Sortino, "Throw Like a Girl?"

Stage 3 kids have a true understanding of the Golden Rule: "Do unto others as *you would have them do unto you.*" Even if someone were to steal from you, you shouldn't act that way toward them. As one eleven-year-old boy reasoning at Stage 3 said, "There's no end to revenge."

Stage 3 morality is more forgiving. Rules are important but can be flexibly applied to take extenuating circumstances into account. Kids are also now capable of performing good deeds without expecting a reward. If they can make a practice of doing one good deed for one person a day or paying a compliment to one person every day, doing good deeds for the sake of making others happy will become a habit—part of their character.

At Stage 3, kids understand the concept "character" as describing the kind of person we are. They can imagine their own character as something that develops over time and is affected, for good or ill, by the actions they engage in. As one ten-year-old girl said, "You shouldn't sneak out of your room if you're grounded. You might grow up to be someone who lies to people. You might become president and lie." It becomes more important than ever for parents to model good character in their words and deeds.

Brain Changing Note: "Class meetings can be an excellent multipurpose tool for your classroom. This simple strategy of setting aside time for students to discuss classroom issues as a group can yield far-reaching benefits. For example, you can hold class meetings to involve students in important decisions such as 'How should cheating be handled?' or 'What can we do about teasing in our school?' Don't be afraid to let students think about these weighty issues.

"You may be surprised by the thoughtful and creative solutions your students propose. While each teacher and class need to find what works best for them, it is worthwhile to have a weekly time set aside for class meetings. It may require only 20 to 30 minutes, but it will be time well spent" (TeacherVision, 2018).

Stage 4: Responsibility to Society; "I Should Be a Responsible Person and Good Citizen" (13 and Up)

The essence of Stage 4 moral reasoning and how it differs from Stage 3 is illustrated by the following classroom debate among eighth graders regarding "Sharon's dilemma": "What should Sharon do when a store security officer demands the name of her companion and good friend Jill, who has just slipped out of the store with a shoplifted sweater?" The first two teens who spoke totally ignored the issue of stealing and treated the whole issue as a matter of Stage 3 loyalty to a friend:

> First boy: She should say, "I don't know her." She should lie for a friend.
> Girl: I agree. Friendship matters more than a rule. I would value somebody I could talk to a lot more than a material thing like a sweater.

Contrast the moral reasoning of these thirteen-year-olds with that of a boy who is concerned about the far-reaching consequences of an action like stealing:

> Second boy: You can't *live* if everybody goes around stealing. I say that if you lie and don't tell on your friend, you will probably keep that crummy friend who left you standing there in the store. But if you tell and lose that friend,

somewhere along the line you will get some other friends, because I'm sure that one or two people in this world are straight.

Friendship is still important to the second boy, but it's not the only thing that matters. Respecting people's property rights is also important. There's a bigger social issue involved. Stage 4's bigger moral vision sees the society-wide consequences of something like stealing.

At Stage 4, being a responsible person is now a higher priority than just being "nice" or loyal. The Stage 4 thinker realizes that if everyone stole or broke other laws whenever they pleased, society could not exist.

Stage 4 also understands the positive duties of being a good citizen. We are obliged to carry out our responsibilities—to our family, community, employer, and whatever other social group or institution we belong to. If we don't pull our weight, that has consequences. Somebody suffers.

Brain Changing Note: "Take the issue of smoking marijuana in school. A Stage 2 thinker might say, 'Whether you smoke pot in school is your own business. It's no skin off anybody else's nose.' At Stage 3 kids would tend to focus on their parents' or friends' feelings about it. But at Stage 4, kids could identify with the school as a system. They could ask, 'What kind of school would we have if everybody came to class stoned?'" (Lickona, 1983).

Helping Individuals Move from Stage 4 to Stage 5 Moral Reasoning

As long as the social system that Stage 4 believes in is working to protect people's rights and serve the common good, Stage 4 is a perfectly good form of moral reasoning. But what happens if the system isn't working to everybody's benefit?

What would you have done, for example, if you were a citizen living in Nazi Germany, and the system you had always been loyal to said, "Jews are less than persons and shall be treated accordingly"? Or what if you're a white person and your system says, "Racial discrimination is permissible"? Or you're male, and the system says, "Women have to tolerate sexual harassment"? Or there is some other subgroup of human beings that is currently being denied equal justice under the law?

Stage 4 lacks an independent standard, a higher moral principle, by which to evaluate the norms and rules of any given system. That opens the door to grave moral dangers. Throughout human history, social and political systems that are not held accountable to transcendent moral principles have sooner or later perpetrated major abuses of human rights. Sometimes the principles are espoused but not practiced consistently. Certain classes of people are treated as less than fully equal. These ethical inconsistencies continue to this day.

Through history, it's been the voice of principled conscience that has held social systems accountable and forced them to ultimately recognize their failures of justice and correct them. How can we help our children develop into the kind of ethical citizen who helps to create a more just and caring society? Here are five ways:

- Discuss social and moral issues with them—perhaps controversial issues in the local newspaper or nightly news. What stage of moral reasoning is being used by the parties to the conflict? What moral principles are involved? Is there a solution that does justice to all?
- Make your kids aware of organizations that work on behalf of human rights. Choose one you think worthy of supporting and contribute as a family.
- Encourage volunteer work with the potential to stimulate a social conscience. Consider doing such service with your child.
- Model moral courage by taking a public stand for a moral cause, however unpopular, that you believe in.
- Help your children develop future goals such as continuing their education in a way that increases their ability to contribute to society. Remember, the higher moral stages build on the highest stage of logical thinking (formal operational thought). You might want to reread chapter three on psychosocial development. Remember, the higher moral stages build on the highest stage of logical thinking (formal operational thought).

Stage 5: Respect the Rights of Every Person (Young Adulthood and Up)

At Stage 5, there is a new basis for moral decisions: the principle of respect for the universal rights of human persons. Stage 5 thinkers

- believe we should show the greatest respect for all citizens and support laws that protect the rights of *all* people regardless of ethnicity, race, economic status, or any other factor
- can mentally stand outside different social systems and evaluate the extent to which they ensure the human rights of all

- understand that people who agree on the principle of respect for universal rights may disagree on particular moral and political issues—and that respect for human rights includes freedom of conscience as long as the exercise of conscience doesn't violate the rights of another
- believe the end doesn't justify the means; it is not morally permissible to do something wrong (e.g., intentionally take innocent life) in order to achieve a good result (e.g., avoiding some other harm)
- understand the moral basis (i.e., respect for human rights) of the Bill of Rights, the U.S. Constitution, and other documents
- understand, as in Stage 4, that although responsibility generally involves keeping commitments to others, one is not morally bound to keep a commitment that involves violating human rights (e.g., one is not required to obey an unjust law or command)

As previously pointed out, we can stimulate and support young people's progress toward the principled conscience of Stage 5 reasoning by helping them empathize with those who have had their rights violated; discussing controversial moral issues at local, state, federal, and international levels; and talking with them about the importance of being an independent, principled thinker. We can help them recognize the sacred value of all individuals as well as diversity. Allow them to be their own person.

Brain Changing Note: "As evidenced in their Senate testimony and other public statements during the Watergate hearings, nearly all members of the Nixon team seem to have reasoned at stages 3 and 4 as measured by Kohlberg's stages of moral development. Indeed, many of the acts of the Watergate participants were 'right' or at least 'permissible' when viewed from the perspective of these stages. Survey responses of 370 persons not involved in Watergate demonstrate that those who reasoned at stages 3 and 4 agreed with the decisions of the Watergate participants more often than did survey respondents who reasoned at stage 5.

"This was true regardless of whether respondents supported Nixon or McGovern. We can conclude that Watergate happened, in part, because the situational pressures to 'win at all costs' made sense to the stage 3 and 4 persons who comprised the leadership of the Nixon administration. From the perspective of their stage of reasoning, the end justified the means"

(Candee, 1975).

Now that we've looked at Kohlberg's stages of moral reasoning, let's revisit the case of my student Richard and the pregnant teens.

Richard and the pregnant teens provide us with an excellent example of how Kohlberg's moral development stages can guide an intervention. Initially, Richard was operating at Stage 2, "an eye for an eye." Abused by his alcoholic mother, he turned this abuse toward other women, in particular, the pregnant teens, who in his mind had done something "bad."

Therefore, I had to find a strategy to help Richard *affiliate/conform* (Stage 3) with a positive female role model (Susan, the farmer's wife) who would be the antitheses of Richard's problematic mother.

Brain Changing Note: "Stage Three (mutual interpersonal expectations, relationships and interpersonal conformity). In this stage, individuals attempt to live up to what is expected of people close to them or what people generally expect of a good son, brother, friend, etc. Being good is important and includes having good motives and showing concern for others. It also means keeping mutual relationships, via trust, loyalty, respect, and gratitude" (Reimer, Pritchard Paolitto, & Hersh, 1999).

Moving Richard to Stage 3 moral reasoning could also help him to accept the pregnant teens, who were not only students and part of the school but also adolescent girls close to his own age. The job at the horse farm was the perfect strategy because that job utilized his strengths and interests—his love of horses and his kinesthetic intelligence—which was emotionally empowering. Furthermore, the farm was run by a young man and his kind and caring wife, Susan. Of course, Susan's attitude toward Richard was an important prerequisite for his connecting with her. As a result, Richard bonded with Susan, particularly after she knitted him a pair of gloves (note the kinesthetic connection).

Richard's changed attitude toward the teens was simply an extension of his relationship (Stage 3) with Susan. Also, Richard formed a deeper emotional relationship with the teens through their knitting group. Finally, when I discovered Richard knitting a uterus in the teens' classroom, I recognized that he was having a strong Stage 3 moral response.

But note that Richard could move in and out of different stages based on his relationships and interactions with other students and staff. For example, with the pregnant teens, his moral reasoning was at Stage 3; however, with other students, his reasoning could be a mixture of Stage 2, Stage 2/3, or something else. Ultimately, I hoped that the longer Richard experienced Stage 3 moral thinking, the more he would become firmly established in that stage, regardless of the situation or individual.

Finally, the importance of Richard's connection to Susan and the teens was crucial to Richard's overall moral development. In fact, it probably saved him from being removed from our school and sent to a residential treatment program.

Brain Changing Note: "The opportunity to establish The Cluster School developed in June 1974 when a group of teachers, parents and students asked permission to open a new alternative school within Cambridge High and Latin School. The Cambridge school committee approved a summer planning workshop resource person to lead these workshops. He was Harvard's Professor Lawrence Kohlberg, who at the invitation of the parents and with the encouragement of the superintendent of schools began this program.

"By the end of the summer the whole group had spelled out the enrollment, staffing, curriculum, governance and space needs of the new school which they decided to call the 'Cluster School.' The group committed itself to implement Kohlberg's concept of a Just Community School. This approach integrated the Social Studies and English curricula with a program of moral discussions and a governance structure based on a participatory Democracy." (Wasserman, 1978).

Brain Changing Note: See "Dr. Kohlberg's Heinz Dilemma" in the appendix.

Chapter Five

Vocational Intelligence

It Is Never Too Early to Attach a Child's Passion to Their True Intelligence—John Holland (1919–2008)

> I saw the angel in the marble and carved until I set him free.—Michelangelo

Vocational intelligence is a preference or a particular interest toward a certain type of vocation that could develop by way of a hobby or interest in your child's play. The bottom line—it is never too early to connect children's play with their vocational intelligence or interest. This does not mean we should program children into specific vocations at an early age. The world is filled with adults who work in careers chosen by their parents, and who end up hating the decision for the rest of their lives!

However, great learning and intelligence can be experienced when you allow children to focus on activities they are passionate about. Again, *expose* but do not *indoctrinate* professions.

For example, one of the most valuable experiences for many children occurs when professionals give talks in schools about their chosen career. "Bring your child to work day" is another great strategy for children to be exposed to a future profession.

In addition, when the child is exposed to various hobbies, games, and pastimes associated with careers, you are not only attaching a face or a voice to a career, but in my opinion, you are stimulating the emotional midbrain (hippocampus, the site of bonding), which connects to the executive brain centers (cerebral cortex) and higher-order thinking.

Further, perceptive parents need to take the lead by addressing the child's particular multiple intelligence at home as well. For instance, the child who never seems to get enough of nature could be expressing his vocational intelligence as a naturalist. The child who demonstrates a high aptitude for building or taking things apart could end up as a surgeon or auto mechanic. Therefore, parents should consider connecting this interest or personality with environmental classes, nature hikes, and the like. Again, such exposure gives a *face* to the experience, which is an obvious leg up on a potential career.

Brain Changing Note: See chapter 2 on multiple intelligences.

Moreover, I have used vocational assessments based on John L. Holland's research extensively with middle school (CareerExplorer) and high school and college students (Self-Directed Search). Holland was a psychologist and a professor of sociology at Johns Hopkins University. Assessments based on his work explore hobbies as a way to define a student's potential vocational interest/intelligence. In fact, some of my greatest vocational development successes have been with hard-to-reach, at-risk youth such as juvenile offenders. For the first time in juvenile offenders' problematic lives, someone was actually connecting their potential vocational skills or interests to a career and saying, "You can be someone!"

Therefore, your first act—whether you're a parent, guardian, or mentor—should be to use one of these easy-to-apply vocational assessment for yourself. Once your child or student has done so, too, you can try and connect him or her with professionals in their identified vocational interest fields.

Brain Changing Note: Google Holland's vocational assessments before reading any further. A free self-assessment will provide an in-depth personal description of Holland's six vocational types.

Again, regardless of the child's age or circumstance, the wise parent, guardian, or teacher should begin to observe their child in play as a way to connect the vocational intelligence dots. From my perspective, it is never too early to begin to feed into a child's vocational intelligence. It happened with Bill Gates, who started hanging out at a University of Washington computer lab when he was fourteen years old, and to Steven Spielberg, who asked his parents for a camera so he could make family movies at a young age. It just might happen with your child as well!

REALISTIC (THE DOER)

> "In the past, you had to be a big, butch bloke to do this job," he says. "But the entry rules have been altered a bit. While there's still a certain amount of heavy lifting, there are techniques that don't require brute strength. And some of the equipment that we have to lug around is lighter than it used to be." (Arnot, 2008)

The realistic vocational personality expresses their intelligence with their hands, using tools or instruments of all shapes and sizes to express their strong kinesthetic skills.

Brain Changing Note: "Because of their ability with physical objects, they are often good in emergencies. A realistic personality type can deal well with the physical world, which often means they are very independent, practical-minded, strong, aggressive and conservative. They may not have strong communication skills and tend to think in absolutes" (123Test, 2018).

Brain Changing Note: "The cerebellum processes information from the brain and peripheral nervous system for balance and body control. Activities such as walking, hitting a ball and playing a video game all involve the cerebellum. The cerebellum helps us to have fine motor control while inhibiting involuntary movement. It coordinates and interprets sensory information in order to produce fine motor movements. It also calculates and corrects informational discrepancies in order to produce the desired movement" (Bailey, 2019).

In early childhood, the realistic child's mechanical inclinations and physical dexterities will be displayed in a variety of kinesthetic challenges and abilities. For example, in play, anything that allows them to use their hands to build, manipulate, and position things should always be within arm's reach!

In late childhood, parents should indulge their brain with elaborate erector sets, puzzles, or anything that allows them to create or build. They are the neighborhood fix-it kid, to whom everyone goes when they need something repaired or assembled. In fact, their hands may be as advanced as a gifted surgeon's!

Also, this gift should never be taken for granted. When Joey creates something extraordinary from a pile of junk or Janie builds a tree fort, they need to hear compliments for their labors or creations. In other words, when you compliment an action, you invoke all great things within their emotional brain, namely, the chance to bond (hippocampus) with something they are passionate about. Remember, the hippocampus is not only an area of the brain where neurons regenerate, but it also connects to higher areas of the brain.

Brain Changing Note: "The hippocampus has a unique shape, similar to that of a horseshoe. It not only assists with the storage of long term memories, but is also responsible for the memory of the location of objects or people. We would not even be able to remember where our house is without the work of the hippocampus" (Brain Made Simple, 2017).

In addition, children with a realistic vocational personality are highly practical and probably invented the slogan "be real." A word to the wise: when the realistic personality is passionately involved in an activity, a Do Not Disturb sign should be hung in your mind.

Brain Changing Note: Not allowing the realistic child to express his or her intelligence and creative juices could result in *behavioral problems* in school and at home. An excellent alternative school program would be Montessori because many of the school lessons focus on kinesthetic intelligence. Again, to teach children the alphabet or phonemes, Maria Montessori employed sandpaper letters so children could recite the alphabet as they dragged their fingers over the letter.

Also, the realistic personality often exerts a "no fuss, no muss" or "what you see is what you get" personality, and parents and teachers need to honor this personality. Again, the realistic personality requires a school curriculum (such as Montessori) that allows them to use their bodies and hands to express their high kinesthetic intelligence so their creative genius can appear.

Moreover, with the proper support, adolescence can be a period for this student to take their realistic intelligence to a higher level of learning by enrolling either in a technical high school or simply joining clubs or socializing with students who are like minded.

Adolescents who do not have the opportunity for a realistic expression often become disenchanted with school and can be prone to fail both academically as well as socially. During my work as a consultant at a juvenile hall, the one learning modality that appeared in nearly all of my vocational assessments with male and female juvenile offenders was the realistic personality (75 percent). In my opinion, we could save a great deal of taxpayer money and save juveniles the indignity of being locked up by providing this personality with the option to attend a technical high school.

Brain Changing Note: Google Dr. David Sortino, "Getting Practical about the Drop Out Rate and Juvenile Delinquency."

Brain Changing Note: A Washingtom state study showed that 75 percent of adult inmates spend time in a juvenile facility (*Child Trends*, 2015).

Can you attach your child's interests with any of the following vocations?

Archeologist
Audiologist
Architect
Astronaut
Athlete
Babysitter
Chef
Computer Scientist
Driver
Electrical Engineer
Engineer
Farmer/Rancher
Firefighter
Gardener
Information Technologist
Instructional Technologist
Martial Arts Instructor
Mechanic
Mechanical Engineer
Paramedic
Pharmacist
Physical Therapist

Pilot
Police Officer
Veterinarian

1. Describe an incident or age when your child demonstrated a vocational interest toward any of the fields listed above.
2. Research schools, camps, workshops, and books (autobiographies) that support this child's interest.
3. Set up an opportunity for successful individuals associated with your child's vocational interest to meet and talk about their particular occupation. Ask them why or how they became interested in their chosen field and so forth. Better yet, invite them over for dinner.

ARTISTIC (THE CREATOR): NONCONFORMING, ORIGINAL, INDEPENDENT, CHAOTIC, CREATIVE

> Why artists are poor and why we shouldn't be.
> The crucial role artists play in culture, and why it's often under-valued.
> Tools and principles artists have used to thrive.
> Why artists already have the skills needed to make balanced, sustainable lives.
> (Artists U, 2016)

Just as with the realistic personality, we must always remember it will be the artist's emotional midbrain that drives this child to bond (hippocampus) with their creative needs. Nevertheless, since it is the brain's right side (spatial and visual intelligence) that feeds the artistic, it will also be the right side's emotional midbrain or the amygdala that can place their brain into a state of disharmony or fight or flight.

In addition, the artistic personality can be very disorganized, unstructured, and overly spontaneous because it sees and feels the world *spatially* and *kinesthetically*. In short, their creative juices must flow for their creative genius to appear in school and in life.

They will avoid routines at all costs, and adults should be aware that young children with this creative bent will fight you tooth and nail about rules and structure. In fact, this is only their way of expressing their need to be creative.

Again, their emotional highs and lows of their limbic system are only a response to create. The catch-22 of early childhood can create the emotional turmoil, especially if they are placed in a preschool or kindergarten that is not arts oriented. However, if placed in the correct school environment or one that supports an artistic personality, magical and incredible creations can appear in all facets of their life.

Brain Changing Note: "By encouraging creativity and imagination, we are promoting children's ability to explore and comprehend their world and increasing their opportunities to make new connections and reach new understandings" (Duffy, 2006).

Therefore, in early childhood, parents should always have available finger paints, clay, drawing pencils, crayons, and the like for spontaneous discovery. Again, Montessori and Waldorf, school curriculums that integrate the arts, are made for this child. When such children are allowed to combine their sensory and motor skills with their artistic interests, they can develop and prosper to unimaginable levels.

Brain Changing Note: "Babies' brains are amazing powerhouses that appear to grow in response to creative environments. The reason why children learn holistically and heuristically (i.e., experientially) is because they are going through a unique experience—the young brain makes billions of new connections with every bit of knowledge that is taken in, in order to make sense of it. This process is called synaptogenesis and happens most prolifically between the ages of birth to three" (Early Arts, 2017).

As children move from early childhood to late childhood, their cognitive skills become more advanced, and as such it is imperative that parents enroll them in art classes or art camps that invite skill development and problem-solving opportunities supported by an artistic curriculum.

Moreover, choosing the right teacher is critical at all stages, but the need for a truly experienced art teacher is of critical importance for this age group. Remember, late childhood or middle school serves as a critical bridge (Erikson's industry vs. inferiority) to adolescence. Therefore, positive role models should be prominent in every teacher's and parent's playbook.

Brain Changing Notes: "A publication that was put out by the National Committee of State Legislators, 'Reinventing the Wheel: A Design for Student Achievement in the Twentieth Century,' lists an impressive number of benefits provided by arts education. They include:

1. Art can integrate all subject areas in a school.
2. Art provides the possibility for new ways of assessing students.
3. Art excites learners and keeps them in school. (Studies show that dropout levels decrease with the number of art courses taken by students.)
4. Art promotes a developmentally informed perception.
5. Art aids in creative problem solving, decision-making skills, and critical thinking.
6. Art helps promote self-discipline, self-esteem, and self-awareness.
7. Art stimulates cooperative learning and helps multi-cultural understanding." (James, 2002)

Adolescence is the time for skill development and the mastery of artistic skills. As a result, adolescents should keep journals or portfolios to record their feelings or artistic creations on paper or canvas as positive reminders of what they have achieved. In addition, a portfolio should be maintained for potential future enrollment in art school.

Finally, volunteer opportunities related to the arts can allow them to pursue their artistic talents in the real world.

Actor/Performer
Animator
Art Therapist
Artist
Author/Poet
Dance Therapist
Expressive Therapist
Graphic Designer
Librarian/Information Science Technician
Music Therapist
Musician
Painter

1. Describe an incident or age when your child demonstrated a vocational interest toward any of the fields listed above.
2. Research schools, camps, workshops, and books (autobiographies) that support this child's interest.

3. Set up an opportunity for successful individuals associated with your child's vocational interest to meet and talk about their particular occupation. Ask them why or how they became interested in their chosen field and so forth. Better yet, invite them over for dinner.

SOCIAL (THE HELPER): HEALING, NURTURING

> We need to find God, and he cannot be found in noise and restlessness. God is the friend of silence. See how nature—trees, flowers, grass—grows in silence; see the stars, the moon and the sun, how they move in silence. We need silence to be able to touch souls.—Mother Teresa

The *social* vocational interest begins and ends with serving others in a helping or humanistic way. They are the teachers, healers, and counselors of the vocational world.

In early childhood, parents often see in this child a high degree of empathy toward others. Most importantly, parents need to spend time discussing and listening to the social personality's concerns about the emotional aches and pains caused by the cruelty of others. Books and films with *helping themes* are especially reinforcing and healing to this personality.

The social personality needs affirmations of kindness from adults. Avoid the tendency to dismiss this child's feelings and concerns. In fact, words and superficial responses may not satisfy this personality type and will only devalue their caring nature or feelings toward others.

Brain Changing Note: "Research by neuroscientists Shonkoff and Philipps demonstrates that high quality social and cultural experiences are more critical in the early years for the development of healthy brains and well-rounded personalities than at any other time during the rest of childhood and adulthood. These critical experiences include imaginative, creative and cultural opportunities which can help children to build contexts, make meaning and deepen their understanding" (Early Arts, 2017).

Again, these children could become the bedrocks of humanity, and we need to pay close attention to this unique, caring personality. This child needs to express his or her humanity through social service and serving mankind. For example, they can serve as volunteers at retirement communities or taking care of abandoned animals at an animal shelter. We are simply putting a face on their social personalities, placing them in situations with professionals who, like themselves, have a profound need to create a better world by helping others or animals.

Brain Changing Note: Studies show that 80 percent of doctors pursued a medical profession because they experienced a traumatic event in childhood.

On the school playground, these children are the social butterflies or the child that everyone turns to for support or consul. Developmental psychologist Erik Erikson would define the social personality as industrious when placed in a helping situation.

Brain Changing Note: "Neuroscience has discovered that our brain's very design makes it sociable, inexorably drawn into an intimate brain-to-brain linkup whenever we engage with another person. That neural bridge lets us impact the brain—and so the body—of everyone we interact with, just as they do us. Even our most routine encounters act as regulators in the brain, priming emotions in us, some desirable, others not. The more strongly connected we are with someone emotionally, the greater the mutual force. The most potent exchanges occur with those people with whom we spend the greatest amount of time day in and day out, year after year—particularly those we care about the most" (Goleman, 1995).

Moreover, the strong empathy these children feel toward others leads them to believe that they are able to feel what others feel. And finally, their intense determination to help others motivates an undying belief that they can actually change the world.

Occupations:

Art Therapist
Audiologist
Babysitter
Caretaker
Counselor
Dance Therapist
Educator
Instructional Technician
Martial Arts Instructor
Music Therapist
Nurse

Nutritionist
Physician
Professor
Psychologist
Social Worker
Teacher
Theologian
Trainer (Industry)
Speech-Language Therapist

1. Describe an incident or age when your child demonstrated a vocational interest toward any of the fields listed above.
2. Research schools, camps, workshops, and books (autobiographies) that support this child's interest.
3. Set up an opportunity for successful individuals associated with your child's vocational interest to meet and talk about their particular occupation. Ask them why or how they became interested in their chosen field and so forth. Better yet, invite them over for dinner.

ENTERPRISING (THE PERSUADER): COMPETITIVE, LEADING, SELLING, DOMINATING, PROMOTING, STATUS ORIENTED

> Your most unhappy customers are your greatest source of learning. Success is a lousy teacher. It seduces smart people into thinking they can't lose. Life is not fair; get used to it.—Bill Gates

The *enterprising* vocational type must be in a position to direct others toward self-chosen goals. As toddlers, they may exhibit this personality in less appropriate self-centered ways (terrible twos).

Brain Changing Note: See chapter 3 on Erikson's psychosocial development theory, particularly the stages autonomy vs. doubt and shame and initiative vs. guilt.

In fact, their needs are singular, and whatever it takes to get their needs met knows no boundaries. They learn quickly that selling a cute smile or being superficially social can get their needs met.

In addition, they can be natural leaders, but in their need to lead, they can be overly pushy or aggressive, which can turn other children off, particularly with play dates. Parents must ensure that they learn the art of *sharing and compromise*. Your motto should be *whoever comes into our home or play area should always be treated as a guest*. This motto should be reinforced before every play date.

From a developmental perspective, they could have problems entertaining two levels of social interaction at a time. During early childhood (ages two to seven), they can only entertain one idea or individual at one time, which is first getting their needs met. You can move them to higher cognitive stages by teaching sharing. That is, make them aware of the positive as well as the negative social implications of the enterprising vocational personality through sharing.

Brain Changing Note: "If a kid has trouble playing fair, it is probably not because he does not understand the concept. Rather he simply cannot resist the urge to grab all the cookies and run. Author Steinbeis points out, however, that this finding does not excuse bad behavior. 'Just because the brain is that way doesn't mean it can't be changed,' he says. 'Education and setting a good example can have an enormous impact'" (*Scientific American*, 2012).

In late childhood, their need to make money has them bartering with other children for toys or bargaining with parents for more allowance. At this age, they can be seen holding monthly yard sales, setting up a lemonade stand, or selling the most Girl Scout cookies. Still, it is crucial that parents take the lead and try and redirect their social conscience and appreciating of the value of money to other enterprising experiences, such as opening up a savings account or donating some of their money to needy organizations.

In sports, we often see the enterprising personality totally focused on the need to always *win at all costs*, rather than appreciating the experience and knowledge one can learn from simply participating. Therefore, parents need to reinforce sportsmanship and, again, the beauty of participation.

Brain Changing Note: See John Wooden's excellent book *Game Plan for Life* (2009).

As adolescents, these children have an equally strong need to persuade others and win at all costs, so encourage them to join debate teams or get involved in local political campaigns. Their strong persuasive abilities make them perfectly suited as a babysitter or as a day care worker due to their strong ability to direct and take charge.

Brain Changing Note: Social media, while it connects us to others, may actually lead to greater self-centeredness as people strive to make their "presence" known. Much of social media is "all about me." Overly doting helicopter parents may also be creating greater narcissism in children. Finally, society, with its emphasis on celebrity, appearance, and narcissistic role models and leaders, may be playing a part in the rise in self-centeredness.

Moreover, this vocational type sees itself as having the ability to sell ideas to any and everyone, regardless that *anyone* is not ready or willing to listen. Others see them as having incredible energy, needing attention, and possessing the ability to lead others. Therefore, to satisfy their need to lead and to convince others, they should seek a well-respected position of power in school government or become number one seller in the school's raffle.

Academic Administrator
Administrator
Businessperson/MBA
Communications Specialist
Insurance Salesperson
Investment Banker
Journalist
Lawyer/Politician
Manager
Management Consultant
Marketer/Advertiser
Public Health Worker
Public Policy Creator
Public Relations Worker
Publisher
Real Estate Agent
Retail Salesperson
Salesperson
Stock Broker/Investment Analyst

1. Describe an incident or age when your child demonstrated a vocational interest toward any of the fields listed above.

2. Research schools, camps, workshops, and books (autobiographies) that support this child's interest.
3. Set up an opportunity for successful individuals associated with your child's vocational interest to meet and talk about their particular occupation. Ask them why or how they became interested in their chosen field and so forth. Better yet, invite them over for dinner.

CONVENTIONAL (THE ORGANIZER): PRECISE, EXTREMELY ATTENTIVE TO DETAIL, ORDERLY

> If you want your children to be intelligent, read them fairy tales. If you want them to be more intelligent, read them more fairy tales.—Albert Einstein

As toddlers, the conventional personality demands predictability and organization throughout the home environment. The terrible twos might not be so terrible for these organizers if the home environment is predictable and filled with routines. However, the slightest disorganization can be unsettling to their orderly personalities—that includes meals, bedtime, and other special times.

Brain Changing Note: "Kids' brains are organized differently than those of adults, scientists have learned through a series of brain scans. The workings of children's neural connections are more governed by proximity to one another than is the case in adult brains, said Steven E. Petersen of the Washington University School of Medicine in St. Louis" (Thompson, 2009).

In early childhood, the organizer's room is often immaculate, even if they need to rearrange it on a monthly basis because of their need for order. Parents should see this need as an asset and never complain about this child being overly organized. It is something positive and only their conventional personality defining their needs.

In late childhood, this child will call parents and teachers out on their disorganization. Therefore, to ensure that everyone is on the same page, parents should set up a whiteboard or large monthly calendar to record upcoming activities and events.

Brain Changing Note: Early adolescence (ages ten to twelve) is a good time to build students' skills of organizing and prioritizing information and time management. The opportunities you provide to guide them in using these executive functions also provide the activation to strengthen these networks when they are at *peak neoplastic responsiveness*. As a result of this strengthening, your students will build more skills on route to becoming self-directed learners.

This conventional vocational type is the organizer of their clique, pack, or group, the one who makes all the plans or schedules for activities with friends. In school, they will keep the minutes of every student council meeting. At sporting events, they could be the timekeeper or scorekeeper. Finally, walk into any group or classroom and you will find this personality as chief organizer.

Bottom line—routines will contribute to better grades and overall school performance. They value money and power but only if these assist them in the business or vocational world they try to serve.

Brain Changing Note: Google Dr. David Sortino, "Contracts, Adolescence, and Family Values."

Such children prefer incorporating their organizing skills in business rather than in the arts. They are drawn to such occupations as administrator, clerk, and accountant. You could find them working for the IRS, your school's credit union, the military, or law enforcement.

Below is a list of careers associated with a conventional vocational intelligence.

Academic Administrator
Accountant
Actuary
Administrator
Banker/Investor
Businessperson/MBA
Clerk
Copy Editor
Instructional Technician
Payroll Clerk
Proofreader
Receptionist
Retail Clerk

Secretary
Technical Writer

1. Describe an incident or age when your child demonstrated a vocational interest toward any of the fields listed above.
2. Research schools, camps, workshops, and books (autobiographies) that support this child's interest.
3. Set up an opportunity for successful individuals associated with your child's vocational interest to meet and talk about their particular occupation. Ask them why or how they became interested in their chosen field and so forth. Better yet, invite them over for dinner.

INVESTIGATIVE (THE THINKER): ANALYTICAL, INTELLECTUAL, SCHOLARLY, WITH STRONG WRITING OR VERBAL SKILLS

You know my method. It is founded upon the observation of trifles.—Arthur Conan Doyle

The child displaying an *investigative* personality is constantly trying to figure out how things work or finding a better way to do things. In toddlerhood, they can be roamers or explorers, so be sure to childproof the house and yard. Their strong need to problem solve feeds into exploration and discovery. Further, this could be the type of child who ends up in your cabinets taking off labels on your soup cans because they want to know what is behind the labels!

During early childhood, they will try to figure out how to unlock the backyard gate to escape to greener pastures, which again feeds into problem solving and curiosity. Give them a toy and they will have to take it apart to see how it works. Therefore, provide them with problem-solving games, puzzles, mazes, and the like, or simply teach them how to play chess or other board games as early as possible.

In late childhood, they can take their investigative ways to greater heights, particularly with brainteasers, mind games, Rubik's Cubes, and so forth. Do not be surprised if this behavior carries over to the real world. For example, when you set up a homework schedule, they will try to change it more to their liking, so be patient and flexible. In some ways, they are like the social personality who tries to help others. With this personality, however, they become more interested in *solving the problem* rather than helping others.

On the playground, they are always trying to figure out a better game or how they can get more recess time. Again, try to keep their minds occupied with anything and everything that supports problem solving and, above all, their curiosity.

Brain Changing Note: You can build novelty into teaching new information. Changes in voice, appearance, marking key points in color, variation in font size, movement, outdoor lessons, variations of music, curious photos, unexpected objects (a radish on each desk when students enter the classroom) get the RAS (reactivating system) attentive to admit the accompanying sensory input of lessons that relate to the curious sensory input!

Brain Changing Note: Google Dr. David Sortino, "Electronics and Your Child's Novelty-Seeking Brain."

During the late childhood stage, detective stories rule: the Hardy Boys and Nancy Drew reading series as well as Sherlock Holmes are good for their curious minds because they force them to think outside of the box. Also, such mystery novels are perfectly suitable for the child moving from concrete operational (two ideas) to formal operational thinking (three-plus ideas). In many ways, they are the private eyes, psychologists, and research scientists of the vocational world.

Brain Changing Note: Studies about how curiosity changes the brain to enhance learning revealed three major findings. First, when people were highly curious to find out the answer to a question, they were better at learning that information. Also, investigators found that when curiosity is stimulated, there is increased activity in the brain circuit related to reward. Finally, researchers discovered that when curiosity motivated learning, there was increased activity in the hippocampus, a brain region that is important for forming new memories, as well as increased interactions between the hippocampus and the reward circuit (*Neuroscience News*, 2014).

During adolescence, look for such teens to always question the system or authority if they feel these are dishonest or dysfunctional. This is especially true in the family because they will often try to solve everyone's problems, including their own. Further, because they are constantly trying to problem solve or find a better solution to family rules and boundaries, you should consider establishing a behavior contract, if only to keep them in check

Brain Changing Note: Google Dr. David Sortino, "Contracts, Adolescence, and Family Values."

They will excel in science and mathematics or in any other courses that tap into their need to problem solve. As for careers, they are often successful in a medical laboratory. Their attraction is not so much a successful end result but rather *the journey of discovery*.

They see themselves as analytical, intelligent, and very skeptical, with good academic skills rather than social skills. Others might see them as highly introverted and introspective. In the world of multiple intelligence, they often demonstrate an intrapersonal intelligence or reflective learning style. At all costs, they must avoid professions that require persuading others, since that would only be a distraction and waste of energy to their high problem-solving skills.

Brain Changing Note: "Getting into the brain is like getting into an exclusive nightclub where only the glamorous few are selected. Once inside, another gatekeeper, stress, determines what makes the cut to enter the upper VIP lounge in the prefrontal cortex—that valuable 13% of cerebral architecture where our highest and emotional reflection takes place" (Willis, 2016).

For this vocational type to experience professional happiness and success, they must be allowed to use their great analytical, technical, and scientific skills in writing or speaking. This great need comes from the desire to understand others, but in a problem-solving way.

Typical vocational careers:

Actuary
Computer Scientist
Economist
Engineer
Finance Officer
Lawyer
Mathematician
Pharmacist

Physician/Medical School Professor
Professor (all fields)
Psychiatrist
Psychologist
Scientist
Statistician
Surgeon

1. Describe an incident or age when your child demonstrated a vocational interest toward any of the fields listed above.
2. Research schools, camps, workshops, and books (autobiographies) that support this child's interest.
3. Set up an opportunity for successful individuals associated with your child's vocational interest to meet and talk about their particular occupation. Ask them why or how they became interested in their chosen field and so forth. Better yet, invite them over for dinner.

Chapter Six

Thinking

Raising Children's Thinking Skills Increases Intelligence and Learning — Edward de Bono (1933–)

> Thinking is like walking or breathing. There is nothing we need to do about it. There is nothing we can do about it. Any interference with it will only make it awkward and artificial and inhibited by self-consciousness. If you are intelligent, you are a good thinker. If you are not intelligent, that's too bad and you should listen to someone who is. (de Bono, 1985)

Edward de Bono's excellent book *De Bono's Thinking Course* illustrates how learning and intelligence go hand in hand with our ability to think. He recommends his CoRT System, which stands for Cognitive Research Trust, as a valuable tool to enhance your student's thinking skills. Further, *De Bono's Thinking Course* offers parents and teachers excellent exercises to facilitate higher-order thinking and cognitive skills in the home and classroom.

Moreover, life's endless dilemmas often create learning challenges in our relationships and interactions with children and students. In other words, *De Bono's Thinking Course* teaches us how to attach higher-order thinking techniques to our higher brain centers, such as the frontal lobe and our limbic system's hippocampus.

Brain Changing Note: "The frontal lobe is the largest region of the brain and it is more advanced in humans than other animals. It is located at the front of the brain and extends backward to constitute approximately one-third of the total volume of the brain. The frontal lobe, particularly the region located farthest to the front called the prefrontal cortex, is involved in sophisticated interpersonal thinking skills and the competence required for emotional well-being. In general, both the left and right sides of the prefrontal cortex are equally involved in social and interactive proficiency" (Moawad, 2017).

For instance, one of de Bono's brain changing exercises is called the PMI (plus, minus, interesting) method and demonstrates how his thinking method works. According to de Bono, "in conducting a PMI, the adult should deliberately direct the children's attention first toward the (P) plus points, then toward the (M) minus points, and finally toward the (I) interesting points. This is done in a very deliberate and disciplined manner over a period of about 2–3 minutes in all" (de Bono, 1985).

Key de Bono PMI points:

Point #1: "Carrying-out the process is quite easy. What is not easy is to direct attention deliberately in one direction after another when your prejudices have already decided for you what you should feel about an ideal. It is this 'will' to look in a direction that's so important. Once this is achieved, then the natural challenge to intelligence is to find as many P or M or I points as you can. So, there is a switch. Instead of intelligence being used to support a particular prejudice, it is now used to explore the entire subject matter. At the end of the exploration, emotions and feelings can be used to make an unprejudiced decision about the matter. The difference is that the emotions are now applied after the exploration instead of being applied before; thus, preventing exploration."

Point #2: "The I or interesting element of the PMI has several functions. The I category can collect all those points and comments which are either positive or negative. (It might be noted that if a particular point is seen both in the P and also I, it is acceptable that the point can be under both headings. The I also encourages the deliberate habit of exploring matter outside of the judgment framework to see what is interesting about the idea or what it leads to. A simple phrase which is useful for carrying through this I scan is: The thinker is thereby encouraged to expand the idea, rather than just treat it as static."

Point #3: "The I trains the mind to react to the interest inherent in an idea and not just to move judgment feelings about the idea. A thinker should be able to say: I do not like your idea but there are these 'interesting aspects to it . . .' It is a common enough experience that this sort of reaction is highly usual."

Point #4: "Because the PMI seems so very simple, its effectiveness should not be underestimated. I have seen it used to turn a fiercely emotional meeting from prejudices toward consideration of expansion of the subject. Once perception is directed in a certain direction, it cannot help but see, and once something is seen, it cannot be unseen."

Point #5: "The key is practice. Practice doing the PMI yourself and practice demanding it of others. It can be a simple shorthand instruction. The strangeness of the lettering is important in order to give focus. Mere exhortation to someone to look at the good points and bad points is much too weak a process to be effective."

Point #6: "One 13-year-old girl told how at first she thought the PMI was very artificial, since she already knew what she felt about a subject. She then told how, when she had, nevertheless, put points down under P and M and I, she found herself reacting to what she put down and her feeling changed. That is exactly what one would hope to achieve. Once an idea had been thought and put down under any of the headings, that idea cannot be 'unthought' and it will come to influence the final decision." (de Bono, 1985)

For example, de Bono's method asked a class of thirty ten- to eleven-year-olds if they should be paid five dollars for going to school. Children were organized into groups of five. After three minutes, a spokesperson for each group presented their answers. The children's PMI responses were the following:

- The bigger boys would beat them up and take the money.
- Parents would not give presents or pocket money.
- The school would raise its prices for meals.
- Who decides how much each age level should receive?
- There would be quarrels about the money and strikes.
- From what source would the money come?
- There would be less money to pay teachers.

At the conclusion of the exercise, de Bono asked the class *again* if they would like to receive five dollars for going to school. Whereas all thirty students had previously liked the idea, now twenty-nine of them had reversed their view and disliked the idea.

According to de Bono, "teachers noticed that the students' responses to the PMI approach helped them stand back and look at the questions differently. Some students commented that their 'interesting points' were not just black and white but more gray, especially when you think of all the interesting ways to answer the question."

De Bono writes, "They said they felt smarter after they used the PMI thinking method or that it works better when nobody can make up their mind!"

Furthermore, de Bono describes the PMI method as the *spectacle method*, or similar to giving a nearsighted person the appropriate glasses so that the person can see things more clearly or have a different view of the situation. In other words, the thinking tools become glasses allowing students to see a problem more clearly. We then react to what we see (de Bono, 1985).

De Bono's exercises can help individuals think outside of the box. That is, instead of looking at problems from only *two sides*, de Bono's PMI method challenges students to look at *three sides* to come up with a response or again label the response *plus*, *minus*, or *interesting*.

In my opinion, the strength of the CoRT System is its link to *cognitive development* and *formal operational thinking*, or the ability of students to entertain three-plus ideas or concepts at one time. For example, classroom teachers are confronted on a daily basis with multiple student cognitive stages that can contradict prescribed school curriculums or lessons. Therefore, it makes sense for teachers and parents to refer to de Bono's brain-changing methods to stimulate students' cognitive development. (See chapter 1 on cognitive development for additional information.)

Brain Changing Note: "I've spent my life trying to undo habits—especially habits of thinking. They narrow your interaction with the world. They're the phrases that come easily to your mind, like: 'I know what I think,' or 'I know what I like,' or 'I know what's going to happen today.' If you just replace 'know' with 'don't know,' then you start to move into the unknown. And that's where the interesting stuff happens" (Humans of New York, 2015).

In order to confirm the effectiveness of de Bono's CoRT System, I personally conducted de Bono's PMI exercise with fifth grade public school students. Below are the students' responses.

Grade five: ages eleven and twelve, fifteen boys and fourteen girls. The socioeconomic makeup of the fifth graders was 60 percent lower socioeconomic (reduced and free lunches), 30 percent lower–middle socioeconomic, and 10 percent middle socioeconomic. The school's racial makeup was 40 percent Hispanic, 40 percent white, and 20 percent African American.

Should Students Be Paid Five Dollars for Going to School?

Plus Responses

- I could buy more video games.
- I could buy better clothes.
- I could save up to go to Disneyland.
- I could save up for a dirt bike.
- I can buy a new computer.

Minus Responses

- There would be less money for school supplies.
- No money for field trips.
- Less money for hot lunches.
- No money for the library.

Interesting Responses

- You could give money to teachers who work hard.
- You could hire more teacher aides to help in the classrooms.
- Buy more computers for the computer lab.
- You can donate money to the library for books.
- Pay the janitor more money because of how hard he works.

Whereas 20 out of 25 had previously liked the idea, it now appeared that 23 out of 25 had completely reversed their view and now disliked the idea.

Another de Bono PMI example asked, "Should all cars be painted yellow?"

Plus Responses

- They would be easier to see on the roads.
- They would be easier to see at night.
- No problem in deciding what color you wanted.
- No waiting to get the color you wanted.

- Easier for the manufacturer to decide color and order.
- The dealer would need less stock.
- It might take the macho element out of car ownership.
- Cars would tend to become transport items.

Minus Responses

- Boring.
- Difficult to recognize our car.
- Very difficult to find your car in a parking lot.
- Easier to steal cars.
- The abundance of yellow cars might tire the eyes.
- Car chases would be difficult for the police.
- Accident witnesses would have a harder time.
- Restriction of your freedom to choose color.
- Some paint companies might go out of business.

Interesting Responses

- Interesting to see if people appreciated the safety factor.
- Interesting to see whether attitudes toward cars changed.
- Interesting to see if trim acquired a different color.
- Interesting to see if this was enforceable.
- Interesting to see who would support the suggestions.

Brain Changing Note: All cognitive learning activities are geared toward pushing students to work through different problems and stimuli. The goal is to get them thinking and applying problem-solving strategies without the use of preparation or steps that lead to an answer. You want to craft activities that will make your student apply logic, creativity, and close examination on the spot to produce an answer. Cognitive learning essentially relies on five principles: remembering, understanding, applying, evaluating, and creating.

Note to reader: After I completed de Bono's thinking exercises with the students, I sent home this chapter to parents of the students who participated. The parents found they could successfully employ de Bono's PMI exercises with day-to-day dilemmas that often came up with their children. Problems ranging from excessive computer and cell phone time to cleaning their rooms seemed to benefit from discussions using de Bono's PMI exercise.

For additional information about de Bono's thinking course, readers can purchase *De Bono's Thinking Course*.

Chapter Seven

Neurofeedback

*How Brain Training Can Increase
Your Child's Learning and Intelligence*

> The literature, which lacks any negative study of substance, suggests that EEG biofeedback [neurofeedback] therapy should play a major therapeutic role in many difficult areas. In my opinion, if any medication had demonstrated such a wide spectrum of efficacy, it would be universally accepted and widely used. (Frank Duffy, MD, neurologist, Harvard Medical School professor, head of the Neuroimaging Department at Boston Children's Hospital, quote in Brain Works, 2018)

Neurofeedback began in the late 1950s and early 1960s with the work of both Joe Kamiya at the University of Chicago and Barry Sterman at UCLA. Since then, it has grown in use. For the past five years, neurofeedback has been my major approach to support the brain changing concept. Although I continue to assess clients to determine multiple intelligence, cognitive development, vocational intelligence, and so on, it has been neurofeedback that has solidified my practice. In other words, simply identifying a child's particular learning style, cognitive development, or vocational intelligence can be a fruitless journey if the child's *learning brain* is out of control or deregulated.

However, when a parent or teacher connects this book's previous chapters to the use of neurofeedback, I believe he or she can dramatically add another important dimension to the brain changing concept.

I was skeptical that neurofeedback could actually work. I was not very computer literate, and neurofeedback required providers to rely on computers for brain training.

Brain Changing Note: "The distinguishing feature of neurofeedback is that it initiates learning at a neurological level. We are training brain behavior, for which the child does not particularly feel responsible, and to which he may not feel strongly connected. But when brain behavior is normalized, the child's behavior follows. And, eventually, even the child senses that life has become more manageable, without any additional effort on his part" (Steinberg & Othmer, 2014).

My practice (Educational Consulting and Testing and the Neurofeedback Institute) employed proven behavioral and educational assessments to support clients with a variety of learning or cognitive issues. However, missing from my practice was the support needed to address more serious issues, such as ADHD, reactive attachment disorder (RAD), and performance anxiety (for athletes, test takers, and others). Students with these issues sought additional help from me. In short, I was at a crossroads with my practice.

A twelve-year-old girl provided me with the missing information to take the brain changing concept to a higher level. The child had been adopted from Korea after spending ten months in an orphanage of more than six hundred children. Abandonment at two had seriously affected her socially (RAD) and academically (fear of failure). Her bedroom walls still showed the scars of her anger. Her parents tried art, talk therapy, nutritional programs, schools specializing in the arts, but her problems persisted.

I read a parent's article about neurofeedback's success with an adopted ten-year-old girl who exhibited similar problems as my client (Google Dr. David Sortino, "Teaching Students with Reactive Attachment Disorder"). I received further insight from a TV documentary regarding neurofeedback. I learned that neurofeedback techniques would not only help my twelve-year-old client but would also address a variety of other childhood learning disorders, including ADHD, ADD, autism, and more.

I was further convinced when I read that the American Academy of Pediatrics (2012–2013) identified neurofeedback as the number one alternative to medication for ADHD. A month later, I enrolled in neurofeedback training.

My practical neurofeedback training began when a practitioner attached several electrodes to my scalp. Electrodes receive brain waves that are projected back to a computer, allowing clinicians to monitor EEG (electroencephalogram) brain waves.

Brain Changing Note: "An electroencephalogram (EEG) detects electrical activity in your brain using small sensors (electrodes) attached to your scalp. Your brain cells communicate via electrical impulses and are active all the time, even when you're asleep. This activity shows up as wavy lines on an EEG recording" (Mayo Clinic, 2018).

First and foremost, *neurofeedback is not biofeedback*, which is a treatment technique that incorporates instruments to measure physiological responses in a person's body (hand temperature, sweat gland activity, breathing rates, heart rates, blood pressure, brainwave patterns) (Amen, 2001). Instead, neurofeedback is a process that first requires placing several electrodes on the scalp and one or two electrodes on the earlobes.

Then EEG (electroencephalograph) equipment provides real-time, instantaneous audio and visual feedback to the subject about his or her brainwave activity. No electrical current is put into the brain. The brain's electrical activity is simply relayed to the computer, the same way a radio receives radio waves.

Brain Changing Note: "Neurofeedback works by providing feedback to the brain so it can heal itself through neuroplasticity. This is done through sound, lights, computer games and even sometimes vibrating cushions or teddy bears. Neurofeedback is similar to a vocal coach listening to you sing and recording it, or giving you suggestions or positive feedback, also called operant conditioning. There are some methods of neurofeedback that produce the needed frequency to heal your brain: Neurofeedback works by providing feedback to the brain so it can heal itself through neuroplasticity" (Stoler, 2014).

Ordinarily, we cannot reliably influence our brainwave patterns because we lack awareness of them. However, when we can see a representation of our brainwave activity on a computer screen, a few thousandths of a second after shifts occur, it gives us the ability to influence and change these brain patterns through the process of *operant conditioning*, a technique used to shape behavior through positive and negative reinforcement (Google B. F. Skinner and operant conditioning). In a word, neurofeedback practitioners are now able to recondition and retrain the brain through this feedback system.

Brain Changing Note: Another key aspect of neurofeedback is the *skill learning model*, which addresses another critical factor called *self-regulation*. That is, the brain's essential skill, and it benefits from the information we provide in the building of that skill—particularly whenever that skill is deficient.

Brain Changing Note: Over the period of a thirty-minute neurofeedback session, the brain will have an opportunity to self-regulate about two thousand times.

At first, the changes are short lived, but these gradually become more engrained. With continuing neurofeedback, coaching, and practice, improved brain functioning can be seen in most people, and the changes can become permanent. Electrode placements are based on quantitative EEG brain mapping assessments in relationship to the International 10/20 System of Electrode Placement (Marzbani et al., 2016). Moreover, neurofeedback treatment reliably results in many improvements in mental, emotional, and physiological functioning. Areas positively affected vary according to the individual's physiology and deficits.

A wide range of advancements occur as a result of the treatment, including the following:

- Improved focus efficiency and flexibility
- Augmented concentration
- Better organization
- Mood stability
- Improved sleep
- Greater relief from anxiety
- Lessened hyperactivity and restlessness
- Abated depression
- Reduced headaches and seizures
- Enhanced learning capabilities
- Decreased anger
- Diminished overreactions
- Healing from trauma

Improved sensory processing and more accurate perception
More appropriate social interaction
Improved overall sense of well-being (Steinberg & Othrmer, 2014)

"For example, when a child plays a game or watches a movie, the brainwaves are monitored through electrodes attached to the scalp. When playing a game, the individual's brainwaves are monitored by an amplifier and a computer-based instrument that processes the signals and provides proper feedback. Gradually, after a period of time, the brain responds to the continual feedback cues and makes adjustments; consequently, cognitive performance, attention, and self-control improve" (Steinberg & Othmer, 2014).

Brain Changing Note: Neurofeedback is a form of behavioral intervention that aims at improving the skills in the area of intelligence and brain activity (Heinrich, Gevensleben, & Strehl, 2007). Neurofeedback training serves as a mechanism for changing the brain activity and affects people's behavior which benefits ill and healthy people equally. It is a safe and painless method, during which some sensors (called electrodes), are placed on the head (Dempster and Vernon, 2009).

What can neurofeedback do for the child's learning brain? First and foremost, neurofeedback can correct deregulation of the arousal system. For example, ADHD children's brains are overactivated or underactivated. This notable behavior is displayed in irregularities in the EEG. Neurofeedback challenges and modifies the EEG responses and influences brain activation and ultimately the brain's control mechanisms for self-regulation. EEG presents the brain with a continuous stream of challenges. "By feeding back to the client information on what his brain is doing in the last few seconds, the training system challenges the clients brain to adjust, modulate and maintain brain activity within a specific parameter" (Steinberg & Othmer, 2014).

Tommy, age seven, is an excellent example of an ADHD child whose brain was *overaroused and out of control*. After taking meds for the greater part of six months, he was losing weight and not sleeping well. His mother could barely get him out of the house for school without the child exhibiting violent temper tantrums. Any change or transition was met with a similar response. Tommy rarely finished his school assignments.

He was such a behavioral problem that the school's psychologist concluded, after multiple assessments, that continued medication would not be the best remedy to support his ADHD identification. At his IEP (individual education plan) assessment, the planning and placement team (PPT) suggested that his school day be shortened to half days. His mother took him off meds and decided to try neurofeedback for thirty-minute sessions three times a week.

Brain Changing Note: The following ADHD drugs elicited serious psychiatric side effects: methylphenidate (Concerta and Ritalin), lisdexamfetamine (Vyvanse), and atomoxetine (Strattera). Notable were suicidal behaviors, aggression, and hallucination or other manifestation of psychosis. Cardia arrest was associated with methylphenidate and weight loss or arrested growth was reported for three studies (ISMP: Institute for Safe Medication Practices, 2014).

After fifteen sessions, the parents and school staff began to see slight positive behavior changes. "He seemed calmer and more focused," his teacher commented. After twenty sessions, the teacher telephoned me: "Tommy actually finished his morning writing assignment on his own!" She used words like "great progress" to describe the change. Tommy no longer was having tantrums about leaving the house for school. He could transition to other activities at home, and school performance had improved considerably.

After thirty sessions, he could do his homework on his own regardless of whether his younger three-year-old brother was within earshot. We moved to two sessions per week, and at the fortieth session it became one session per week. Thereafter, I only saw him intermittently for tune-up sessions. He continues to exhibit positive behaviors, and the child who would have been placed on medication is leading a normal boy's life, medication free!

Neurofeedback has proved to be effective in reducing brain stress, especially with ADHD children. I deal with individuals from all walks of life who come for neurofeedback due to stress in their everyday lives. This is apparent with individuals in high-stress jobs like CEOs, professional athletes, schoolteachers, and children who are failing in school.

"We have all experienced being stressed. It is not a pleasant experience. The student about to take an exam, the adult preparing for the job interview, the athlete asked to make a shot to win the game, even a man or woman on a first date—all could use neurofeedback training. The problem with stress is that the cause is often external, being stimulated by something from the outside. Conversely, the opposite of stress is what Steinberg describes as a sense of being in the zone, when everything works well and effortlessly" (Steinberg & Othmer, 2014).

For instance, a high-powered athlete describes the zone this way: "It's a very strange feeling. . . . It's as if time slows down, allowing you to see everything clearly . . . you just know that everything about your technique is spot on. It just feels so effortless; it's almost as if you're floating across the track. Every muscle, every fiber, every sinew is working in complete harmony and the end product is that you run fantastically well" (Grout & Perrin, 2006).

The following are some of the athletes and teams who have used neurofeedback to enhance performance: Misty May-Treanor and Kerri Walsh-Jennings, three-time Olympic Gold Medalists in beach volleyball; Eric Shanteau and Jessica Hardy, 2012 U.S. Swim Team Olympic Gold Medalists; Phil Mickelson, World Golf Hall of Famer; the Denver Broncos, AFC division leaders; the Chicago Bears, NFC division leaders; and New York Giants, Super Bowl champions.

Neurofeedback can create dramatically healthy changes in the brain by fostering better integration with the environment. "Our day-to-day activities are spent adapting to different degrees of change: getting up in the morning, going to work, paying bills, attending school, socializing, etc. Our brains must constantly readjust and monitor these transitions. The so-called rampant fluctuations in arousal breach the delicate interplay our nervous systems must maintain to meet inner and outer demands. The adjustments are necessary, but must be automatic" (Steinberg & Othmer, 2014).

The athlete must continuously make adjustments in major competitions to perform at a high level, as does the high-powered CEO dealing with the administration of a major company. The reason for their success is their ability to make adjustments automatically and consistently while maintaining a stable state of calm.

A major challenge for parents and teachers is dealing with children who have difficulty transitioning from one activity to the next. The child who is allowed just sixty minutes watching TV or on a computer game is told to begin homework. The brain is overaroused, resists change, and asks for more TV or computer time.

Brain Changing Note: "Characteristics of Electronic Screen Syndrome in Children: The Child exhibits symptoms related to mood, anxiety, cognition, behavior, or social interaction due to hyperarousal (an overly aroused nervous system) that cause significant dysfunction in school, at home, or with peers.

"Typical signs and symptoms mimic chronic stress or sleep deprivation and can include irritable, depressed, or rapidly changing moods, excessive or age-inappropriate tantrums, low frustration, tolerance, poor self-regulation, disorganized behavior, oppositional–deviant behaviors, poor sportsmanship, social immaturity, poor eye contact, insomnia/non-restorative sleep, learning difficulties, and poor short-term memory. Tics, stuttering, hallucinations, and subtle or overt seizure activity may also occur. Irritability and poor executive functioning occur in most cases and are hallmarks of the disorders" (Dunckley, 2015). Check out Dr. Dunckley's book *Reset Your Child's Brain* for more information.

However, the beauty of neurofeedback is that the "stress reaction" is simply not rewarded. The key has to do with the brain's activation level. That is, when the brain is quietly activated, it is easier to attend to and recognize environmental signals and to adjust one's responses to the demands of the situation. During and after training, children who have had great difficulty transitioning between activities or breaking away from activities show more flexibility and compliance to demands and schedules not of their own choosing.

"In other words, when the child doesn't react to parental requests to shut off the TV or stop playing video games, the child's brain is no longer overaroused but relaxed. Further, when the child's arousal level is regulated, classroom learning becomes more efficient and performance is more consistent (Joseph, 1996; Tranel, 2002). Also with this new self-regulation we get greater focus, accuracy and the ability to improve. More importantly the energy needed to control this over arousal is now available to deal with environmental demands or again, a parent telling the child that TV or computer time is over" (Steinberg & Othmer, 2014).

Neurofeedback can improve flexibility. Flexibility allows adjustments and is a sign of the ability to regulate behavior to achieve desired outcomes. Whether viewing a neurofeedback movie or playing a video game, the client makes automatic adjustments based on the changing conditions of the brain.

Neurofeedback is like driving a car or a bike. You stay on your side of the road; you automatically identify changes in road conditions or oncoming cars. No verbal instruction is needed, yet the brain learns to self-regulate and make correct and spontaneous choices. The brain stays on the straight and narrow. The beauty of neurofeedback is that it teaches the brain by using the brain's own natural tendencies to self-correct yet remain flexible.

A good example of flexibility is a second grade teacher who came for neurofeedback because she was "burnt out" after thirty years of teaching. "Instead of constantly putting out fires, my personality is more flowing and flexible, which carries over to my students, and greater learning is possible," she explained.

Neurofeedback can improve perceptual focusing. A calm brain is a focused, organized brain, which includes experience, knowledge, attention, temperament, and more. In today's world, it is easy to have a cluttered, unfocused, distracted brain. However, by calming the brain, we can create a state of balance that allows us to deal with all the clutter that can permeate our brains. In many ways, the neurofeedback experience is like a clear windshield. There is no dirt or grime on the windshield to prevent you from seeing clearly. Excess brain clutter is the dirt and grime on the windshield of life.

Brain Changing Note: "Concentration, focus and emotional control are keys to achieving optimal performance in all fields. Athletes and business executives are taking advantage of neurofeedback technologies to learn how to utilize the full potential of their minds to reach their peak" (Steinberg & Othmer, 2014).

A fifty-nine-year-old women came for neurofeedback because her world represented all of the above distractions and clutter. She was clearly not seeing the world through a clear windshield. After ten sessions, she experienced dramatic changes in her day-to-day activities. In her weekly knitting group, participants noticed the change in her speed and the accuracy of her knitting. "I was now knitting twice as fast and with greater accuracy! My life has changed. My forgetfulness is no longer a problem. It makes one feel ten years younger!"

Another disorder also affecting the midbrain's limbic system is PTSD, or posttraumatic stress disorder. A vet returning to civilian life after a tour of combat duty cannot immediately separate what is real and not real. Combat experiences can trigger the hot-spot phenomenon, much as stress can trigger children with an attachment disorder. Smells, sounds, and images of combat can trigger the hot spot of PTSD. The success I have experienced with RAD children is very similar to the success of practitioners working with vets afflicted with PTSD.

Brain Changing Note: "A new treatment for PTSD and other brain anomalies may help veterans suffering from Post-Traumatic Stress Disorder (PTSD), which is one of the most common reasons vets apply for VA disability benefits. This treatment, a type of biofeedback, helps train the brain waves in patients who have suffered brain injuries, PTSD, brain tumors and other injuries and impairments that compromise their ability to function and work" (Koven, 2018).

After a number of sessions, I have had ADHD children say, "I feel normal. . . . I do not feel like I am out of control. . . . I am not falling out of my desk. Maybe this is what it is like to be like other kids who never get in trouble." Or the RAD child who says, "I do not have to be perfect all the time. . . ." Further, I have worked with several building contractors who have experienced success from neurofeedback this way: "I feel calmer. . . . I am able to bid on jobs without feeling the stress that I will fail."

Finally, I helped a thirteen-year-old gymnast who experienced severe anxiety prior to major competitions on the balance beam. After twenty neurofeedback sessions, the gymnast placed first in her age group in state competitions. She said, "Now the balance beam looks twice as wide!"

After a bio assessment is made and EEG sites are chosen, the frequency of sessions needs to be determined. I like to compare brain frequencies to running on a treadmill. An individual comes to the gym out of shape. The trainer determines the client's workout level by setting the speed of the treadmill to support the client's specific exercise level or regimen. Too fast and the client will become too tired. Too slow and the client will not receive the full benefit of the workout. However, once the trainer determines the right speed, or with neurofeedback the right frequency, the client can proceed and experience the most optimal exercise.

EEG training frequencies can range from 0.001 hertz (Hz) to 0.40 Hz. For most clients, I start at 0.5 and work down to find the correct frequency. For ADHD clients, the frequency can be higher. As you determine the frequency, the neurofeedback provider checks in with the client every few minutes. If the client is feeling overaroused, the frequency is reduced. If they feel irritable, the frequency is increased. The table gives a list of behaviors associated with arousal indicators. And below are the different states at which our brains operate.

1. **Gamma State (30–100 Hz):** This is the state of hyperactivity and active learning. Gamma state is the most opportune time to retain information. This is why educators often have student audiences jumping up and down or dancing around—to increase the likelihood of permanent assimilation of information. If overstimulated, it can lead to anxiety.

2. **Beta State (13–30 Hz):** Where we function for most of the day. Beta State is associated with the alert mind state of the prefrontal cortex. This is a state of the "working" or "thinking" mind: analytical, planning, assessing, and categorizing.

3. **Alpha State (9–13 Hz):** Brain waves start to slow down when not in thinking mind. We feel more calm, peaceful, and grounded. We often find ourselves in an alpha state after a yoga class, a walk in the woods, a pleasurable sexual encounter, or during any activity that helps relax the body and mind. We are lucid, reflective, and have a slightly diffused awareness. The hemispheres of the brain are more balanced (neural integration).

4. **Theta State (4–8 Hz):** We are able to begin meditation. This is the point where the verbal/thinking mind transitions to the meditative/visual mind. We begin to move from the planning mind to a deeper state of awareness (often felt as drowsy), with stronger intuition and more capacity for wholeness and complicated problem solving. The Theta State is associated with visualization.

Arousal Indicators

Low Arousal	High Arousal
Sedated, slowed down	Agitated, speeded up
Dizziness, nausea	Physical tension, muscle spasms
Sleepy, groggy	Emotional reactivity
Heaviness	Difficulty falling asleep
Sadness, crying	Nightmares
Emotional sensitivity	Hyperactivity, impulsivity
Immature, silly	Eye strain
Lack of deep sleep	Heart palpitations, tachycardia
Difficulty waking	Constipation
Low blood sugar symptoms	OCD, tics

5. Delta State (1–3 Hz): Tibetan monks who have been meditating for decades can reach this in an alert, wakened phase, but most of us reach this final state during deep, dreamless sleep.

Although the computer is the dominant focus of training, feedback and communication among clients, family and teachers, and therapists is essential for success. For example, before I work with ADHD or RAD clients, my initial involvement is to consult with teachers or therapists about the particular child. With parents, it will be an ongoing collaboration of emails, one-on-one meetings, and phone calls. In addition, I often visit the child's classroom and meet with the school psychologist's team for further information and consultation. In short, I cannot experience success with a child without the support and information provided by staff and parents.

In addition, I employ several intake forms and procedures before taking on a client, whatever their age. For children, it may be IEP assessments, doctors' reports, and QEEGs (quantitative electroencephalography).

Finally, an extensive bio assessment is filled out covering the client's personal history. During the first meeting, much is discussed about what neurofeedback entails, such as making a commitment to attend thirty- to forty-minute sessions, most often two times a week. I usually space the sessions one day apart to give me additional information about changes. For ADHD children, I often see them two to three times a week (Monday, Wednesday, Friday), and based on the client's success we can move to once weekly.

While I am attaching electrodes, I almost always have the child paper to draw, paint, or color on. The artwork serves as a way to measure the effects of neurofeedback, almost like a pretest.

Brain Changing Note: "As neurofeedback establishes modulated arousal, people tend to become, more goal-oriented and less tangential. Impulsive reactions to urgencies and crises give way to concentrated awareness of the truly relevant and important aspects of tasks, events, and people. There is a reduction in compulsive preoccupation and an enhanced integration of verbal and nonverbal messages" (Steinberg & Othmer, 2014).

Brain Changing Note: For additional information, see the following books: *ADD: The 20 Hour Solution* (Steinberg & Othmer, 2014) and *A Symphony in the Brain* (Robbins, 2008).

Brain Changing Note: Find the latest in neurofeedback research, see Othmer (2018).

Appendix

MULTIPLE INTELLIGENCE QUIZ

1. Free multiple intelligence quizzes are available online. These are often only a short survey and give a quick interest inventory for multiple intelligences and not an assessment of intelligence. Usually, a quiz asks around twenty-four questions and will take less than five minutes to complete. Try not to think too hard—just go with your first thought when describing your daily activities and interests. By the end, you may have some new insights into the way you think.

You can also view the following MIDAS (Multiple Intelligence Developmental Assessment Scales) links for additional information concerning self-assessment for children, adolescents, and adults.

- Interview with D. Branton Shearer, http://www.youtube.com/watch?v=MSNVeaiJ-pU
- "Room for Multiple Intelligence in Governor's Reform Plan," and interview with Dr. Shearer on WKSU radio, http://www.wksu.org/news/story/22959
- The MIDAS Profile, on Facebook: https://www.facebook.com/themidas-profile/

DR. KOHLBERG'S HEINZ MORAL DILEMMA

In California, a woman was near death from a special kind of cancer. There was one drug that the doctor thought might save her. It was a form of radium that a druggist in the same city had recently discovered. The drug was expensive to make, but the druggist was charging ten times what the drug cost him to make it. He paid one thousand dollars for the radium and charged ten thousand dollars for a small dose of the drug.

The sick woman's husband, Heinz, went to everyone he knew to borrow the money, but he could only get together about one thousand dollars. He told the druggist that his wife was dying and asked him to sell it cheaper or let him pay later. But the druggist said, "No, I discovered the drug, and I'm going to make money from it." So Heinz got desperate and broke into the druggist's store to steal the drug for his wife.

Questions to consider:

- Should Heinz steal the drug? Why or why not?
- What is to be said for obeying the law in this situation or in general?
- In this situation, law and life come into conflict. How can you resolve the conflict, taking the best arguments for both into account?
- If the husband doesn't love his wife, is he obligated to steal the drug for her? Why or why not?
- Why is it so important to save the woman's life? Would it be as right to steal the drug for a stranger as for his wife? Why?
- Heinz steals the drug and is caught. Should the judge sentence him or should he let him go free? Why?
- Thinking in terms of society, what would be the best reasons for the judge to give him a more or less severe sentence?

From Schraf (1978).

2. PYRAMID OF LEARNING

Verbal Processing, Lecture = 5 percent
Verbal Processing, Reading = 10 percent
Verbal and Visual Processing, Demonstration = 30 percent
Verbal and Visual Processing, Discussion Group = 50 percent
Doing, Practice by Doing = 75 percent

Doing, Teaching Others/Immediate Use of Learning = 90 percent

The above pyramid gives average retention rates after twenty-four hours. Students will only remember 5 percent of a lecture. Interestingly, verbal processing is the major approach in most high school classes. The second level, also associated with verbal processing, is reading, with a 10 percent retention rate. The third level combines verbal and visual processing or the audiovisual and has a 30 percent retention rate.

The fourth level is when students are allowed to have group discussions about what they have learned—the retention increases to a 50 percent rate. The fifth level is called practice by doing and represents a retention rate of 75 percent. Practice by doing occurs when the child is asked to duplicate all the steps in a lesson. Finally, the sixth level, teaching others about what they have learned, represents our highest retention rate at 90 percent (NAT'L, 1960).

Since students' interests, learning styles, abilities, and multiple intelligences will vary, so should the percentages from the Pyramid of Learning (Sortino, 2019).

THE BAT EXPERIMENT (REIMER, PRITCHARD PAOLITTO, & HERSH, 1999)

Another experiment to distinguish between the different cognitive stages is to ask a group of ten- and eleven-year-olds to classify the following animals into groups:

Bat Cow Robin Hawk Dog

The majority of concrete operational students, ages seven to ten, will say *walking and flying* or *two legs or four legs*. They see the world logically and concretely, or from two perspectives at one time. However, a small percentage of this age group see other categories. They know that a bat can fly, yet it is also a mammal. This age group has the ability to see abstract categories and can classify the groups by species. The ability to classify the group into species is a major step up from concrete operational thinking. Instead of entertaining two ideas at one time, these students can entertain three ideas or formal operations. Teachers discover that even after they have taught the seven-to-ten age group about species, three to four weeks later those same students, who are thinking at concrete operations, tend to forget the more complex categories and still classify the animals as walking or flying.

Note, however, that when a teacher brought in a live bat to support the bat experiment, five weeks later 100 percent of the students classified bats as mammals.

Bibliography

123Test. (2018). Realistic personality type. Retrieved from https://www.123test.com/realistic-personality-type/

Abuse, N. I. (2006). *Anabolic steroid abuse.* Washington, DC: US Department of Health and Human Services, National Institutes of Health.

Age of Montessori. (2018). Your child's developmental "windows of opportunity." http://ageofmontessori.org/your-childs-developmental-windows-of-opportunity/

Ainsworth, M. D. S., Blehar, M. C., Waters, E., & Wall, S. (1978). *Patterns of attachment: A psychological study of the strange situation.* Hillsdale, NJ: Erlbaum.

Alberta Education. (2013). Take ten—Teaching tools for LD & ADHD. https://www.canlearnsociety.ca/resources/adhd-ld-resources/teaching-tools-for-ld-adhd/

Amen, D. (2019). *Neurofeedback.* Orange County, CA.

American Academy of Pediatrics. (2012–2013). *Evidence-based child and adolescent psychosocial interventions.* San Rafael, CA: Author.

Americans for the Arts (2012). Art students out-perform non-art students on SAT (average points better on SAT's by arts students). https://www.americansforthearts.org/sites/default/files/pdf/get_involved/advocacy/research/2011/sat_artsed11.pdf

Anvari, S. H., Trainor, L. J., Woodside, J., & Levy, B. A. (2002). Relations among musical skills, phonological processing, and early reading ability in pre-school children. *Journal of Experimental Child Psychology, 83,* 111–30.

Armstrong, T. (2009). *Multiple intelligence in the classroom* (3rd ed.). Alexandria, VA: Association for Supervision & Curriculum Development.

Arnot, C. (2008, March). Heat seeker. *Guardian.* Retrieved from https://www.theguardian.com/money/2008/mar/15/workandcareers.publicsectorcareers

Artists U. (2016). Making your life as an artist. Retrieved from http://www.artistsu.org/making#.XV21-mRKiM8

Association Montessori International of the United States. (2017). *Primary guide.* Alexandria, VA: Author.

Assouline, S. & Lupkowski-Shoplik, A. (1999).*Developing math talent: A comprehensive guide to math education for gifted students in elementary and middle school.* Waco, TX: Prufrock.

Bibliography

Atkinson, R. C., & Shiffrin, R. M. (1971). *The central processes of short-term memory.* Palo Alto, CA: Institute for Mathematical Studies in the Social Sciences, Stanford University.

Australia Department of Social Services. (2017). Brain development: teenagers. Retrieved from https://raisingchildren.net.au/pre-teens/development/understanding-your-pre-teen/brain-development-teens

Bailey, R. (2019). Anatomy of the cerebellum and its function. ThoughtCo. Retrieved from https://www.thoughtco.com/anatomy-of-the-brain-cerebellum-373216

Banks, D. (2016). What is brain plasticity and why is it so important? *The Conversation.* Retrieved from http://theconversation.com/what-is-brain-plasticity-and-why-is-it-so-important-55967

Barkho, G. (2016, June). Why are millennials putting off marriage? Let me count the ways. *Washington Post.* Retrieved from https://www.washingtonpost.com/news/soloish/wp/2016/06/06/why-are-millennials-putting-off-marriage-let-me-count-the-ways/?noredirect=on

Baron-Cohen, S. (2003). *The essential difference: The truth about the male and female brain.* New York: Basic Books.

Barry, N., Taylor, J., & Walls, K. (2002). The role of the fine and performing arts in high school dropout prevention. In R. J. Deasy (Ed.), *Critical links: Learning in the arts and student academic and social development* (74–75). Washington, DC: Arts Education Partnership.

Bloom, B. S. (1976). *Human characteristics and school learning.* New York: McGraw-Hill.

Bohn, S. & Danielson, C. (2017). Just the facts: Poverty in California. Retrieved from https://www.ppic.org/publication/poverty-in-california/

Bonta, J., Wallace-Capretta, S., Rooney, J., & McAnoy, K. (2002). An outcome evaluation of a restorative justice alternative to incarceration. *Contemporary Justice Review, 5,* 319–38.

Bonwell, C. C., & Eison, J. A. (1991). Active learning: Creating excitement in the classroom. *ASHE-ERIC Higher Education Reports.* Retrieved from https://files.eric.ed.gov/fulltext/ED336049.pdf

Booth, J., Wood, L., Lu, D., Houk, J. C., & Bitan, T. (2007). The role of the basal ganglia and cerebellum in language processing. *Brain Research, 1133*(1), 136–44.

Boyes, K. (2016). *Teacher Matter Magazine, 16.*

Brain Made Simple. (2017). Hippocampus. Retrieved from https://brainmadesimple.com/hippocampus.html

Brain Works. (2018). Solutions. Retrieved from https://brainworksneurotherapy.com/neurofeedback-solutions

Brainy Quotes (2019). San Francisco, CA.

Brannon, E. J., & Van Der Wale, G. (2001). Ordinal numerical knowledge in young children. *Cognitive Psychology, 43,* 53–81.

Bratton, S. C., Ray, D., Rhine, T., & Jones, L. (2005). The efficacy of play therapy with children. *Professional Psychology: Research and Practice, 36*(4), 376–90.

Brown, M. (2009, December). How driving a taxi changed London cabbie's brains. *Wired.* Retrieved from https://www.wired.com/2011/12/london-taxi-driver-memory/

Brodie, T. (2018). San Francisco, CA: Scribd.

Buckley, W. E., Yesalis, C. E., Friedl, K. E., Anderson, W. A., Streit, A. L., & Wright, J. E. (1988). Estimated prevalence of anabolic steroid use among H.S. seniors. *JAMA, 260*(23), 3441–45.

Building a Master Memory. (2010). Memorizing poetry. Retrieved from http://memoryskills.blogspot.com/2010/07/memorising-poetry.html

Burton, J. M., Horowitz, R., & Abeles, H. (2000). Learning in and through the arts: The question of transfer. *Studies in Art Education, 41,* 228–57.

Butterworth, B. (1999). *What counts: How every brain is hardwired for math.* New York: Free Press.

Buzan, T. (1989). *Use both sides of your brain* (3rd ed.). New York. Penguin.

Buzzell, K. (1998). *The children of Cyclops: The influence of television viewing on the developing human brain.* San Francisco, CA: Association of Waldorf Schools of North America.

Cahill, L. (2005, May). His brain, her brain. *Scientific American, 292,* 40–47.

Calvin, W. (2004). *A brief history of the mind: From apes to intellect and beyond.* New York: Oxford University Press.

Candee, D. (1975). The moral psychology of Watergate. *Journal of Social Issues, 31*(2), 183–92.

Carter, T., Hardy, C. A., & Hardy, J. C. (2001). Latin vocabulary acquisition: An experiment using information-processing techniques of chunking and imagery. *Journal of Instructional Psychology, 28,* 225–28.

Centers for Disease Control. (2017). *National youth risk behavior survey.* Atlanta, GA: Author.

Chapman, C. (1993). *If the shoe fits: How to develop multiple intelligences in the classroom.* Thousand Oaks, CA: Corwin Press.

Cherry, K. (2018). Industry vs. inferiority in psychosocial development: Stage four of psychosocial development. About.com. Retrieved from https://www.verywellmind.com/industry-versus-inferiority-2795736

Child First. (2016). 16 characteristics of kinesthetic and tactile learners. Retrieved from https://child1st.com/blogs/resources/113559047-16-characteristics-of-kinesthetic-and-tactile-learners?_pos=1&_sid=75269dffa&_ss=r

Child Trends. (2015). Retrieved from https://www.childtrends.org/

Childwise. (2015). Research highlights for children's public safety: #84.

Chugani, H. T. (1998). A critical period of brain development: Studies of cerebral glucose utilization with PET. *Preventive Medicine, 27*(2), 184–88.

Cooper, H. (2003). Summer learning loss: The problems and some solutions. LD Online. Retrieved from http://www.ldonline.org/article/8057/

Cowan, N. (2001). The magical number 4 in short-term memory: A reconsideration of mental storage capacity. *Behavioral and Brain Sciences, 24*(1), 87–114.

Cowan N. (2005). *Essays in cognitive psychology: Working memory capacity.* New York: Psychology Press.

Cozolino, L. (2017). *The neuroscience of psychotherapy: Healing the social brain.* New York: W. W. Norton.

Data Back. (2011). Executive summary. Urban Child Institute. Memphis, TN.

Deans, E. (2015, November). Iron, dopamine and ADHD. *Psychology Today.*

de Bono, E. (1985). *De Bono's Thinking Course.* New York: Facts on File.

de Bono, E. (2018). De Bono thinking systems. Retrieved from http://www.debonothinkingsystems.com/

Dempster, T., & Vernon, D. (2009). Identifying indices of learning for alpha neurofeedback training. *Applied Psychophysiology and Biofeedback, 34*(4), 309–18.

Developmental Education. (2014). What happens to children when parents fight. Retrieved from https://www.developmentalscience.com/blog/2014/04/30/what-happens-to-children-when-parents-fight

Dewar, G. (2018). Is your child securely attached? Understanding the Strange Situation test. Retrieved from https://www.parentingscience.com/strange-situation.html

Dewey, G. C., Benedek, E. P., & Benedek, D. M. (1987). Characteristics of adolescents charged with homicide: Review of 72 cases. *Behavioral Sciences, 5*(1), 11–23.

Diamond, M., & Hopson, J. (1998). *Magic trees of the mind: How to nurture your child's intelligence, creativity, and healthy emotions from birth through adolescence.* New York: Dutton.

Dohmen, B. (2018, June). Is intuition a form of intelligence? *Forbes.*

Droz, M., & Ellis, L. (1996). *Laughing while learning: Using humor in the classroom.* Longmont, CO: Sopris West.

Druckerman, P. (2012). *Bringing up bébé.* New York: Penguin.

Duffy, B. (2006). *Supporting creativity and imagination in the early years.* Oxford: Oxford University Press.

Dunckley, V. (2015). *Reset your child's brain: A four-week plan to end meltdowns, raise grades, and boost social skills by reversing the effects of electronic screen-time.* Navato, CA: New World Library.

Dunlosky, J., & Rawson, K. A. (2005). Why does rereading improve miscomprehension accuracy? Evaluating the levels-of-disruption hypothesis for the rereading effect. *Discourse Processes, 40*, 37–56.

Dunlosky, J., Rawson, K. A., Marsh, E. J., Nathan, M. J., & Willingham, D. T. (2014). Improving students' learning with effective learning techniques: Promising directions from cognitive and educational psychology. *Psychological Science in the Public Interest, 14*(1), 4–58.

Dweck, C. (2015, January). The secret to raising smart kids. *Scientific American.*

Early Arts. (2017, March). Creativity in early brain development. Retrieved from https://earlyarts.co.uk/blog/creativity-in-early-brain-development

Economist. (2017, November). Why would-be parents should choose to get married. Retrieved from https://www.economist.com/special-report/2017/11/23/why-would-be-parents-should-choose-to-get-married

Education Source. (2012). Understanding school discipline in California: Perceptions and practice. Retrieved from https://edsource.org/wp-content/publications/edsource_discipline_survey_09-10_v6.pdf

Education World. (2018). Calling all grandparents: Senior volunteers transform schools. Retrieved from https://www.educationworld.com/a_admin/admin/admin355.shtml

Edutopia. (2016a). Multiple intelligences. Retrieved from https://www.edutopia.org/multiple-intelligences-research

Edutopia. (2016b). What works in public education. Retrieved from https://www.edutopia.org/editors-note-grassroots-education-reform

Edwards, L. (2003). Writing instruction in kindergarten: Examining an emerging area of research for children with writing and reading difficulties. *Journal of Learning Disabilities, 36*(2), 136–48.

Encyclopedia.com. (2018). Beatles, the. Retrieved from https://www.encyclopedia.com/people/literature-and-arts/music-popular-and-jazz-biographies/beatles

Endocrine Society. (2009). Endocrine-disrupting chemicals. Retrieved from https://www.endocrine.org/advocacy/priorities-and-positions/edc

Erikson, E. (1968). *Identity, youth, and crisis.* New York: W. W. Norton.

Evans, K. R. (2013). Doing time in ISS: A performance of school discipline. *Counterpoints, 440*, 123–53.

Evans, K. R., & Lester, J. N. (2013). Restorative justice in education: What we know so far. *Middle School Journal, 44*(5), 57–63.

Farrell-Kirk, R. (2007). *Tips on understanding and encouraging your child's artistic development.* Washington, DC: Author.

Feinstein, S. (2009). *Inside the teenage brain: Parenting a work in progress.* Lanham, MD: Rowman & Littlefield.

Felder, R., & Solomon, B. (2018). *Learning styles and strategies.* Raleigh, NC: North Carolina State University.

Ferguson, L. (2017, May). Benefits of reading to spot. *Tufts Now.* Retrieved from https://now.tufts.edu/articles/benefits-reading-spot

Ferris, J. (2011, December). Cache cab: Taxi drivers' brains grow to navigate London's streets. *Scientific American.* Retrieved form https://www.scientificamerican.com/article/london-taxi-memory/

Fisch, S. M., Truglio, R. T., & Cole, C. F. (1999). The impact of Sesame Street on preschool children: A review and synthesis of 30 years' research. *Media Psychology, 1,* 165–190.

Fiske, R. D. (Ed.). (1999). *Champions of change: The impact of the arts on learning.* Washington, DC: President's Committee on the Arts and the Humanities.

Forbes. (2012, November). How far apart should you space your kids? Retrieved from https://www.forbes.com/sites/learnvest/2012/11/08/how-far-apart-should-you-space-your-kids/#a6fc70e1b768

Franceschini, S., Gori, S., Ruffino, M., Pedrolli, K., & Facoetti, A. (2012). A causal link between visual spatial attention and reading acquisition. *Current Biology, 22*(9), 814–19.

Fulbright, R. K., Jenner, A. R., Mencl, W. E., Pugh, K. R., Shaywitz, B. A., Shaywitz, S. E., . . . Gore, J. C. (2008). The cerebellum's role in reading: A functional MR imaging study. *American Journal of Neuroradiology, 20*(10), 1925–30.

Gaab, N., & Zuk, J. (2017, May). Is there a link between music and math? *Scientific American Mind.* Retrieved from https://www.scientificamerican.com/article/is-there-a-link-between-music-and-math/

Gable, S. (2000). Creativity in young children. University of Missouri Extension. Retrieved from https://extension2.missouri.edu/gh6041

Gabreelli, J., & Bundge, S. (2017). The story of poverty. *Scientific American Mind, 28,* 54–61.

Gabriel, J. N., & Lester, N. (Eds.). *Performances of research: Critical issues in K–12 education.* New York: Peter Lang.

Gaddes, W. (1985). *Learning disabilities and brain function: A neuropsychological approach* (2nd ed.). New York: Springer Verlag.

Gardner, H. (1983). *Frames of the mind: The theory of multiple intelligence.* New York: Basic Books.

Gavin, M. (2015). Safe exploring for toddlers. Kids Health. Retrieved from https://kidshealth.org/en/parents/exploring.html

Gazzaniga, M. (Ed.) (2008). *Learning, arts, and the brain.* New York: Dana Press.

Geller, S., & Walker, B. (2012, June). BPA Bombshell: Industry database reveals 16,000 foods with toxic chemical in packaging BFA. Environmental Working Group.

Gladwell, M. (2008). *Outliers: The story of success.* New York: Little, Brown.

Goldberg, E. (2001). *The executive brain: Frontal lobes and the civilized mind.* New York: Oxford University Press.

Goleman, D. (1995). *Emotional intelligence: Why it can matter more than I.Q.* New York: Bantam.

Golemen, D. (2006). *Emotional intelligence.* London: Bantam.

Gomez, M. (2010, November). Art therapy helps children cope with tragedy. CBS New York. Retrieved from https://newyork.cbslocal.com/2010/11/04/art-therapy-helps-children-cope-with-tragedy/

Gottfredson, G. D., Jones, E. M., & Holland, J. L. (1993). Personality and vocational interests: The relation of Holland's six interest dimensions to five robust dimensions of personality. *Journal of Counseling Psychology, 40*(4), 518–24.

Gross, G. (2014, September). Your baby's brain, part 3: Windows of opportunity. *Huffington Post*. Retrieved from https://www.huffpost.com/entry/your-babys-brain-part-3-windows-of-opportunity_b_5806108

Grout, J., & Perrin, S. (2006). *Mind games: Inspirational lessons from the world's finest sports stars*. Washington, DC: Capstone.

Haberman, C. (2016, October). The unintended consequences of taking a hard line on school discipline. *New York Times*. Retrieved from https://www.nytimes.com/2016/10/03/us/the-unintended-consequences-of-taking-a-hard-line-on-school-discipline.html

Hallam, S. (2002). The effects of background music on studying. In R. J. Deasy (Ed.), *Critical links: Learning in the arts and student academic and social development* (pp. 74–75). Washington, DC: Arts Education Partnership.

Hallam, S. (2005). *Enhancing learning and motivation through the life span*. London: Institute of Education, University of London.

Hallam, S., & Prince, V. (2000). *Research into instrumental music services*. London: Department for Education and Employment.

Hamann, D., Bourassa, R., & Aderman, M. (1990). Creativity and the arts. *Dialogue in Instrumental Music Education, 14*, 59–68.

Hamann, D., Bourassa, R., & Aderman, M. (1991). Arts experiences and creativity scores of high school students. *Contribution to Music Education, 14*, 35–47.

Hammond, C. (2007). Neurofeedback for the enhancement of athletic performance and physical balance. *Journal of the American Board of Sport Psychology, 1-2007*, article 1.

Hannaford, C. (2011). *The dominance factor*. Salt Lake City: Great River Books.

Harland, J., Kinder, K., Lord, P., Stott, A., Schagen, I., & Haynes, J. (2000). *Arts education in secondary schools: Effects and effectiveness*. Slough, UK: National Foundation for Educational Research.

Harms, W. (2011, January). Writing about worries eases anxiety and improves test performance. *University of Chicago News*.

Hart, L. (1983). *Human brain and human learning*. New York: Longman.

Hawkins, J., & Blakeslee, S. (2004). *On intelligence*. New York: Times Books.

Heinrich, H., Gevensleben, H., & Strehl, U. (2007). Annotation: Neurofeedback—train your brain to train behavior. *Journal of Child Psychology and Psychiatry, 48* (1), 3–16.

Hetland, L. (2000a). Learning to make music enhances spatial reasoning. *Journal of Aesthetic Education, 34*(3/4), 179–238.

Hetland, L. (2000b). Listening to music enhances spatial-temporal reasoning: Evidence for the Mozart effect. *Journal of Aesthetic Education, 34*, 105–48.

Hirsh, R. (2010). *Bodily/kinesthetic intelligence in the early childhood classroom*. New York: Prentice Hall.

Howard, K. (1999). *Do brain cells regenerate?* Princeton, NJ: Princeton University Press.

Huitt, W. (1997). Cognitive development: Applications. *Educational Psychology Interactive*. Retrieved from http://www.edpsycinteractive.org/topics/cogsys/piagtuse.html

Huitt, W., & Hummel, J. (2003). Piaget's theory of cognitive development. *Educational Psychology Interactive*. Retrieved from http://www.edpsycinteractive.org/topics/cognition/piaget.html

Hull, J. (2011). Time in school: How does the US compare? Center for Public Education.

Humans of New York. (2015, July). Retrieved from https://www.facebook.com/humansofnewyork/posts/ive-spent-my-life-trying-to-undo-habitsespecially-habits-of-thinking-they-narrow/1029622267111873/

Hyde, K. L., Lerch, J., Norton, A., Forgeard, M., Winner, E., Evans, A. C., & Schlang, G. (2009). The effects of musical training on the structural brain development. *Annals of the New York Academy of Sciences, 1169*, 182–86.

Institute for Safe Medication. (2018). Horsham, PA.

Ipatenco, S. (2019, June). The 22 best moral stories for kids. Care.com. Retrieved from https://www.care.com/c/stories/4048/the-22-best-moral-stories-for-kids/en-au/

James, V. (2002). Arts and their relationship to adolescent development. Online Waldorf Library. Retrieved from https://www.waldorflibrary.org/articles/680-arts-and-their-relationship-to-adolescent-development

Kaiser, D. A., & Othmer, S. (2000). Effect of neurofeedback on variables of attention in a large multi-center trial. *Journal of Neurotherapy, 4*(1), 5–15.

Karen, R. (1999). *The naturalist intelligence: An introduction to Gardner's eighth intelligence.* Thousand Oaks, CA: Corwin Press.

Karpicke, J. (2016, June). A powerful way to improve learning and memory. *Psychological Science Agenda.* Retrieved from https://www.apa.org/science/about/psa/2016/06/learning-memory

Keane, J. (2006). *The big book of children's reading lists.* Westport, CT: Libraries Unlimited.

Kelly, M. (2017). How to analyze problems using logical mathematical intelligence. Thought Company. Retrieved from https://www.thoughtco.com/logical-mathematical-intelligence-profile-8094

Kim, J. S., & Quinn, D. M. (2013). The effects of summer reading on low-income children's literacy achievement from kindergarten to grade 8: A meta-analysis of classroom and home interventions. *Review of Educational Research, 83*(3), 386–431.

Kimura, D. (1992). Sex differences in the brain. *Scientific American, 267*, 119–24.

Kohlberg, L. (1981). *The philosophy of moral development: Moral stages and the idea of justice.* San Francisco: Harper & Row.

Kovan, S. (2018). Veteran Treatments: PTSD Interventions. *Healthcare 6*(3): 94.

Kuhn, D., Langer, J., Kohlberg, L., & Haan, N. S. (1977). The development of formal operations in logical and moral judgment. *Genetic Psychology Monographs, 95*, 97–188.

Lahey, J. (2016, January). The steep costs of keeping juveniles in adult prisons. Atlantic. Retrieved from https://www.theatlantic.com/education/archive/2016/01/the-cost-of-keeping-juveniles-in-adult-prisons/423201/

Langholt, A. (2017). Ring! Your intuition is calling. *Brain World.* Retrieved from https://brainworldmagazine.com/ring-intuition-calling/

Lawson, A. E., & Wollman, W. T. (1976). Encouraging the transition from concrete to formal cognitive functioning: An experiment. *Journal of Research in Science, 13*(5), 413–30.

LeBoutillier, N., & Marks, D. F. (2003). Mental imagery and creativity: A meta-analytic review study. *British Journal of Psychology, 94*, 29–44.

Lewin, T. (2006, September). Perfect's new profile, warts and all. *New York Times.*

Lewis, M. (2003). *Money ball.* New York: W. W. Norton.

Lickona, T. (1983). *Raising good children: From birth through the teen years.* New York: Bantam Books.

Lindamood, C., & Lindamood, P. (1975). *Auditory discrimination in depth, book 1: Understanding the program.* Boston: Teaching Resources Corp.

Lloyd, K. M. (2018). *An analysis of Maria Montessori's theory of normalization in light of emerging research in self-regulation.* (Unpublished doctoral dissertation). Oregon State University, Corvallis, OR.

Lockey, R. (2016). What are formal operational thinking examples? Quora. Retrieved from https://www.quora.com/What-are-formal-operational-thinking-examples

Loomans, D., & Kolberg, K. (1993). *The laughing classroom: Everyone's guide to teaching.* Tiburon, CA: H. J. Kramer.

Luckerson, V. (2015, April). More women aren't having children, study finds. *Time.* Retrieved from https://time.com/3774620/more-women-not-having-kids/

Macquire, E. A., Frith, D. C., & Morris, R. G. M. (1999, October). The functional neuroanatomy of comprehension and memory: The importance of prior knowledge. *Brain, 122,* 1839–50.

Macrae, F. (2012, April). Bring water into exams to improve your grades. *Science Daily.* Retrieved from https://www.sciencedaily.com/releases/2012/04/120417221621.htm

Main, M., & Solomon, J. (1986). Discovery of an insecure-disorganized/disoriented attachment pattern. In T. B. Brazelton & M. W. Yogman (Eds.), *Affective development in infancy* (pp. 95–124). Westport, CT: Ablex.

Marshall, D. B., English, D. J., & Stewart, A. J. (2001). The effects of fathers on father figures on child behavioral problems in families referred to child protective services. *Child Maltreatment, 6*(4), 290–99.

Marzbani H., Marateb H. R., & Mansourian M. (2016). Neurofeedback: A comprehensive review on system design, methodology and clinical applications. *Basic Clinical Neuroscience 7*(2): 143–58. doi: 10.15412/J.BCN.03070208.

Mayo Clinic. (2015). Performance enhancing drugs: Know the risks. Retrieved from https://www.mayoclinic.org/healthy-lifestyle/fitness/in-depth/performance-enhancing-drugs/art-20046134

Mayo Clinic. (2017). Reactive attachment disorder: Symptoms and causes. Retrieved from https://www.mayoclinic.org/diseases-conditions/reactive-attachment-disorder/symptoms-causes/syc-20352939

Mayo Clinic. (2018). EEG (electroencephalogram). Retrieved from https://www.mayoclinic.org/tests-procedures/eeg/about/pac-20393875

Miller, G. (1956). The magical number seven, plus or minus two: Some limits on our capacity for processing information. *Psychological Review, 63,* 81–97.

Millman, R. P. (2005, June). Excessive sleepiness in adolescents and young adults: Causes, consequences, and treatment strategies. *Pediatrics, 115,* 1774–86.

Mischel, W., Shoda, Y., & Rodriguez, M. L. (1989). Delay of gratification in children. *Science, 244*(4907), 933–37.

Moawad, H. (2017). Parts of the brain associated with thinking skills. LiveStrong. Retrieved from https://www.livestrong.com/article/145593-parts-of-the-brain-associated-with-thinking-skills/

Montessori Kids Brandon. (2017). Montessori classrooms. Retrieved from http://montessorikidsbrandon.com/education/tag/montessori-classrooms/

Montessori, M. (2008). *The Montessori method.* Radford, VA: Wilder.

Muftuler, L. T., Bodner, M., Shaw, G. L., & Nalcioglu, O. (1999). fMRI of Mozart effect using auditory stimuli. Abstract presented at the seventh meeting of the International Society for Magnetic Resonance in Medicine, Philadelphia.

Myers, J. (1997). *Our stolen future: Are we threatening our fertility, intelligence and survival?* New York: Plume.

National Geographic Guide. (2016). *Complete guide to brain health.* Washington, DC: Author.

National Reading Panel. (2000). *Teaching children to read: An evidence-based assessment of the scientific research literature and its implications for reading instruction.* Washington, DC: National Institute of Child Health and Human Development.

National Training Laboratories. (2018). Learning pyramid. Retrieved form https://www.fitnyc.edu/files/pdfs/CET_Pyramid.pdf

Neuroscience News. (2014, October). How curiosity changes the brain to enhance learning. Retrieved from https://neurosciencenews.com/curiosity-memory-learning-neuroscience-1388/

Northwestern University. (2012, March). Diagnosis of ADHD on the rise. *Science Daily.* Retrieved from https://www.sciencedaily.com/releases/2012/03/120319134214.htm

O'Connor, C. (2015). Practicing reality: Play in the Montessori environment. Unpublished master's thesis. University of Wisconsin, River Falls.

OECD. (2007). *Understanding the brain: The birth of a learning science.* Paris: Author.

Orenstein, P. (1994). *Schoolgirls: Young women, self-esteem and the confidence gap.* New York: Doubleday.

Ornstein, R., & Thompson, R. (1984). *The amazing brain.* Boston: Houghton Mifflin.

Othmer, S. (2018). Evidentiary basis for infra-low frequency neurofeedback. EEGInfo.com. Retrieved from http://www.eeginfo.com/research/pdfs/Evidentiary-Basis-for-ILF-Neurofeedback.pdf

Pearce, J. C. (1977). *Magical child.* New York: E. P. Dutton.

Pearce, J. C. (1986). *Magical child matures.* New York: Bantam.

Piaget, J. (1932). *The moral judgment of the child.* New York: Free Press.

Pinker, S. (2002). *The blank slate: The modern denial of human nature.* New York: Viking.

Pilcher, H. (2004). Brain machine interfaces. *Nature, 431,* 993–96.

Poldrack, R. (2009). Russell Poldrack: May I have your attention? The brain, multitasking and information overload. Project Information Literacy.

Poldrack, R. (2011, November). Multitasking: The brain seeks novelty. *Huffington Post.* Retrieved from https://www.huffpost.com/entry/multitasking-the-brain-se_b_334674

Rabkin, N., & Redmond, R. (2004). *Putting the arts in the picture: Reframing education in the 21st century.* Chicago: Columbia College.

Raths, J. (2002, Autumn). Improving instruction. *Theory into Practice, 41*(4), 233–37.

Reay, D. (2001). "Spice girls", "nice girls", "girlies", and "tomboys": Gender discourses, girls' cultures and femininities in the primary classroom. *Gender and Education, 13*(2), 153–67.

Reggio, R. R. (2017, July). Are we all becoming more self-centered? *Psychology Today.* Retrieved from https://www.psychologytoday.com/us/blog/cutting-edge-leadership/201707/are-we-all-becoming-more-self-centered

Reimer, H., Merz, F., Ehlers, T., & Remer, H. (1995). The effect of schooling on the development of fluid and crystallized intelligence. *Intelligence, 21*(3), 279–96.

Reimer, J., Pritchard Paolitto, D., & Hersh, R. H. (1999). *Promoting moral growth: From Piaget to Kohlberg.* Prospect Heights, IL: Waveland Press.

Renata, R. (2018, June). Uses of classical conditioning in the classroom. Classroom. Retrieved from https://classroom.synonym.com/uses-of-classical-conditioning-classroom-7603215.html

Restak, R. M. (2001). *The secret life of the brain.* Washington, DC: Dana Press.

Restak, R. M. (2003). *The new brain: How the modern age is rewiring your mind.* New York: Rodale.

Robbins, J. (2008). *A symphony in the brain: The evolution of the new brain wave biofeedback* (rev. ed.). New York: Grove Press.

Roberts, P., & Kellough, D. (2003). *A guide for developing interdisciplinary thematic units* (3rd ed.). Englewood Cliffs, NJ: Prentice Hall.

Robertson, R. (2007, July/August). The meaning of marks: Understanding and nurturing young children's writing development. *Child Care Exchange, 176*, 40–44.

Roediger, H., & Finn, B. (2009, October). Getting it wrong: Surprising tips on how to learn. *Scientific American Mind*. Retrieved from https://www.scientificamerican.com/article/getting-it-wrong/

Roediger, H., & Finn, B. (2010). The pluses of getting it wrong. *Scientific American Mind, 21*(1), 38–41.

Rosenthal, R., & Jacobson, L. (1968). *Pygmalion in the classroom: Teacher expectations and pupils' intellectual development.* New York: Holt, Rinehart and Winston.

Rosin, H. (2010, July/August). The overprotected kid. *Atlantic*.

Rotbart, H. A. (2012). How to spend more quality time with your child. *Parents*. Retrieved from https://www.parents.com/parenting/better-parenting/positive/quality-time/

Rotigel, J. V., & Lupkowski-Shoplik, A. (1999). Using talent searches to identify and meet the educational needs of mathematically talented youngsters. *School Science and Mathematics, 99*, 330–37.

Rowen, D., Biggs, M., Watkins, N., & Rasinski, T. (2007). Choral reading theater: Bridging accuracy automaticity. *Journal of Teacher Action Research*, 53–69.

Rubin, B. S. (2011). Bisphenol A: An endocrine disruptor with widespread exposure and multiple intelligence. *Journal of Steroid Biochemistry and Molecular Biology, 127*(1–2), 27–34.

Rubin, B. S. (2015). *Cognitive processes.* Thousand Oaks, CA: Corwin Press.

Russell, P. (1979). *The brain book.* New York: E. P. Dutton.

Sadker, D., & Sadker, M. (1994). *Failing at fairness: How our schools cheat girls.* Toronto: Simon & Schuster.

Sandseter, E. B. H. (2007). Categorising risky play: How can we identify risk-taking in children's play? *European Early Childhood Educational Research Journal, 15*(2), 237–52.

Schacter, D. L. (1996). *Searching for memory: The brain, mind, and the past.* New York: Basic Books.

Schank, R. C. (1990). *Tell me a story: Narrative and intelligence.* Evanston, IL: Northwestern University Press.

Schlaug, G., & Gaser, G. (2003). Gray matter differences between musicians and nonmusicians. *Annals of the New York Academy of Sciences, 999*, 514–17.

Schmidt, S. R. (1995). Effects of humor on sentence memory. *Journal of Experimental Psychology: Learning, Memory and Cognition, 20*, 953–67.

Schonberg, C. (2013, April). Psychology classics: Piaget's stages of cognitive development. Psychology in Action. Retrieved from https://www.psychologyinaction.org/psychology-in-action-1/2013/04/21/piagets-stages-of-cognitive-development

Schraf, P. (1978). *Readings in moral education.* Minneapolis: Winston Press.

Schwartz, B. L., Son, L. K., Kornell, N., & Finn, B. (2011). Four principals of memory improvement: A guide to improving learning efficiency. *International Journal of Creativity & Problem Solving, 21*(1), 7–15.

Schwarz, A. (2013, December). The selling of attention deficit disorder. *New York Times*.

Schwarz, A., & Cohen, S. (2013, March). ADHD seen in 11% of US children as diagnoses rise. *New York Times*.

Science Daily. (2010, May). Books in home as important as parent's education in determining children's educational level. Retrieved from https://www.sciencedaily.com/releases/2010/05/100520213116.htm

Scientific American. (2012, July). Young brains lack skills for sharing. Retrieved from https://www.scientificamerican.com/article/young-brains-lack-skills-sharing/

Scientific Learning. (2016). Fast ForWord reading language program. Retrieved from https://www.scilearn.com/products/fast-forword

Shadmehr, R., & Holcomb, H. H. (1997). Neural correlates of motor memory consolidation. *Science, 277*(5327), 821–25.

Shearer, B. (2004a). Multiple intelligence theory after 20 years. *Teachers College Record, 106*, 2–16.

Shearer, B. (2004b). *Stepping stones: A teacher's workbook for the multiple intelligence*. Kent, OH: Zephyr.

Sheffield, L. J. (1994). The development of gifted and talented mathematics students and the National Council of Teachers of Mathematics Standards (Report No. RBDM 9404). Storrs: National Research Center on the Gifted and Talented, University of Connecticut.

Sherna N. (2012). Teenagers' life balance revealed 17 hours weekly for T.V. and another 17 hours for internet. *Independent* (UK).

Shiver, E. (2001). Brain development and mastery of language in the early childhood years. IDRA Newsletter. Retrieved from https://www.idra.org/resource-center/brain-development-and-mastery-of-language-in-the-early-childhood-years/

Sigle-Rushton, W., & McLanahan, S. (2004). Father absence and child wellbeing: A critical review. In D. P. Moynihan, L. Rainwater, & T. Smeeding (Eds.), *The Future of the family* (pp. 116–55). New York: Russell Sage Foundation.

Sirkin, A. (2013, January). The complete guide on how to build a crystal radio—plus how they work. Wonder How To. Retrieved from https://steampunk.wonderhowto.com/how-to/complete-guide-build-crystal-radio-plus-they-work-0141117/

Skiba, Russel. (2006). Are zero tolerance policies effective in the schools? American Psychological Association Zero Tolerance Task Force. Retrieved from https://www.apa.org/pubs/info/reports/zero-tolerance.pdf

Sortino, D. (2011). *The promised cookie: No longer angry children*. Bloomington, IN: Author House.

Sousa, D. A. (2005). *How the brain learns to read*. Thousand Oaks, CA: Corwin Press.

Sowell, E. R., Thompson, P. M., Holmes, C. J., Jernigan, T. L., & Toga, A. W. (1999). In-vivo evidence for post-adolescent brain maturation in frontal and striatal regions. *Nature: Neuroscience, 2*, 859–61.

Sparks, S. (2013, May). Children's spatial skills seen as key to math learning. Education Week. Retrieved from https://www.edweek.org/ew/articles/2013/05/15/31learning.h32.html

Squire, L. R., & Zola-Morgan, S. (1988). Memory: Brain systems and behavior. *Trends in Neuroscience, 11*(4), 170–75.

Stansfield, S. (2012). *Teach your child to read with movement, fun and games*. N.p.: Xlibris.

Steinberg, L. (2005). Cognitive and effective development in adolescence. *Trends in Cognitive Development, 9*(2), 69–74.

Steinberg, M., & Othmer, S. (2014). *ADD: The 20-hour solution*. Bandon, OR: Robert Reed.

Steinfeld, M. B. (2018). Bonding is essential for normal infant development. UCDavis Medical Center. Retrieved from https://health.ucdavis.edu/medicalcenter/healthtips/20100114_infant-bonding.html

Steiner, R. (1995). *The kingdom of childhood*. Dornech, Switzerland: Anthroposophic Press.

Stoler, D. R. (2014, October). Neurofeedback: How does it work? *Psychology Today*. Retrieved from https://www.psychologytoday.com/ca/blog/the-resilient-brain/201410/neurofeedback-how-does-it-work

Strauss, L. (2011, October). My class size matters. *Huffington Post*. Retrieved from https://www.huffpost.com/entry/class-size_b_1025760

TeacherVision. (2018). Class meetings. Retrieved from https://www.teachervision.com/classroom-management/class-meetings

Telegraph Reporter. (2015, March). The Mozart effect: Can classical music really make your baby smarter? *Telegraph*. Retrieved from https://www.telegraph.co.uk/news/health/children/11500314/Mozart-effect-can-classical-music-really-make-your-baby-smarter.html

Thompson, A. (2009). Child brains organized differently than adult brains. Live Science. Retrieved from https://www.livescience.com/3616-child-brains-organized-differently-adult-brains.html

Tokuhama-Espinosa, T. (2011). *Mind, brain, and educational science: A comprehensive guide to the new brain-based teaching*. New York: W. W. Norton.

Turner, A. (2014). How meditation changes your brain frequency. MindBodyGreen. Retrieved from https://www.mindbodygreen.com/0-12491/how-meditation-changes-your-brain-frequency.html

University of California–San Diego. (2005, March). Autism linked to mirror neuron dysfunction. EurekaAlert! Retrieved from https://www.eurekalert.org/pub_releases/2005-03/uoc--alt032905.php

Vaughn, K., & Winner, E. (2000). SAT scores of students who study the arts: What we can and cannot conclude about the association. *Journal of Aesthetic Education, 34*(3/4), 77–89.

Wadsworth, B. (1984). *Piaget's theory of cognitive and affective development* (3rd ed.). New York: Longman.

Wahlstrom, K., Dretzke, B., Gordon, M., Peterson, K., Edwards, K., & Gdula, J. (2014). Examining the impact of later high school start times on the health and academic performance of high school students: A multisite study. College of Education and Human Development, University of Minnesota.

Wakefield, J. (2015, May). Children spend six hours or more a day on screens. *BBC News*.

Wasserman, E. (1978). Implementing Kohlberg's "just community concept" in an alternative high school. In P. Schraf (Ed.), *Readings in moral education* (pp. 164–73). Minneapolis: Winston Press.

WebMD. (2018). Reactive attachment disorder. Retrieved from https://www.webmd.com/mental-health/mental-health-reactive-attachment-disorder#1

Wedge, M. (2012, May). Why French kids don't have ADHD. *Psychology Today*. retrieved from https://www.psychologytoday.com/us/blog/suffer-the-children/201203/why-french-kids-dont-have-adhd

Weinberger, N. M. (2004). Music and the brain. *Scientific American, 291*, 89–95.

Weisburg, D. (2006). What does Batman think about Sponge Bob: Understanding of the fantasy/fantasy distinction. *Cognition, 101*(1), B9–18.

Willis, J. (2016, November). Want children to pay attention? Stimulate their curiosity. NPJ/Science of Learning. Retrieved from https://npjscilearncommunity.nature.com/users/20252-judy-willis/posts/13446-want-children-to-pay-attention-stimulate-their-curiosity

Wilson, A. (2015). *How to increase gray matter in the brain*. Decater, GA: Inner Light.

Wilson, L. (2018a). The eighth intelligence—naturalistic intelligence. The Second Principle. Retrieved from https://thesecondprinciple.com/optimal-learning/naturalistic-intelligence/

Wilson, L. (2018b). The nine intelligence—existential or cosmic smarts. The Second Principle. Retrieved from https://thesecondprinciple.com/optimal-learning/ninth-intelligence-existential-cosmic-smarts-2/

Winerman, L. (2005). The mind's mirror. American Psychological Assiciation. Retrieved from https://www.apa.org/monitor/oct05/mirror

Wixted, J. T. (2004). The psychology and neuroscience of forgetting. *Annual Review of Psychology, 55*, 235–69.

Wolfson, A., & Carskadon, M. (1998). Sleep schedules and daytime functioning in adolescents. *Child Development, 69*, 875–87.

Wong, A. (2015, June). The *Sesame Street* effect. *Atlantic*. Retrieved from https://www.theatlantic.com/education/archive/2015/06/sesame-street-preschool-education/396056/

Wooden, J. (2009). *Game plan for life*. New York: Bloomsbury.

World Health Organization. (2009). *Infant and young child feeding*. Geneva: Author.

Zhang, X., Koponen, T., Räsänen, P., Aunola, K., Lerkkanen, M. K., & Nurmi, J. E. (2012). Linguistic and spatial skills predict early arithmetic development via counting sequence knowledge. *Child Development, 85*(3), 1091–1107.

Index

abstract thinking, 14, 15. *See also* formal operations
action as stimulus, 11
ADD (Auditory Discrimination in Depth Program), 34
ADD (Steinberg and Othmer), 118
ADHD (attention deficit hyperactivity disorder), 4, 35, 111–112, 116, 118
alpha state of arousal, 117
ambivalent children, 56
American Academy of Pediatrics, 108
Anan of Nigeria, 39
animal classification experiment, 18
anticipatory set, xv
anxious children, 56
arousal states of the brain, 116–118
artistic personality, 84–87, 86
Artists U, 84
assessment of career types, xvi
Association Montessori International, 29
athletes and neurofeedback, 112–113, 116
attachment disorders, 5, 55. *See also* emotional attachments
attentional system of children, 56–57
attention deficit hyperactivity disorder (ADHD), 4, 35, 111–112, 116, 118
Auditory Discrimination in Depth Program (ADD), 34
authority figures, 67–68
autism, 40

autonomy vs. doubt and shame stage, ix, 55–56, 89
avoidant-insecure children, 56

baby talk, 7
Bartlett, Sir Frederic, 35
bat experiment, 18, 123–124
The Beatles, 41
Berry, Joy, 68
beta state of arousal, 117
biofeedback, 109
bonding, 54–55, 56. *See also* emotional attachments
brain plasticity, xiii
brain structure. *See also* arousal states of the brain; neurofeedback: of adolescents, 16–17; of autistic individuals, 40; cerebellum, 12, 40, 81; cerebral cortex, 79; comparison of adults and children, 92; frontal lobe, 99; heart's connection to, 9; hippocampus, xv, xvi, 54, 79, 82, 84, 95, 99; mirror neurons, 39; prefrontal cortex, 96, 117; reading process and, 10; right brain and left brain, 41; social personality and, 88; synaptogenesis, 85
breastfeeding, 54

careers matched to multiple intelligences: interpersonal intelligence, 44–45; intrapersonal intelligence, 47; logical-

mathematical intelligence, 30; music intelligence, 42; naturalist intelligence, 50, 51; spatial intelligence, 34
careers matched to personality types. *See also* vocational development theory: artistic personality, 86; conventional (organizer) personality, 93–94; enterprising (persuader) personality, 91; investigative (thinking) personality, 81–97; naturalist intelligence, 50; realistic personalities, 83–84; social (helper) personality, 88–89
Carson, Johnny, 26, 44
cerebellum, 4, 12, 81
cerebral cortex, 79
character development, 71
childlessness, 61
classical music, 8
classification experiment, 123–124
class meetings, 72
classroom engagement: naturalist intelligence activities, 50
Cluster School, 77
cognitive conflict. *See* disequilibration/disequilibrium
cognitive development stages. *See also* formal operations: about, xv, 1–2; bat experiment, 123–124; concrete operational thinking stage, 2, 123–124; Huitt's findings on classroom stages and, 2–3; preoperational stage, 8–12; sensory and motor stage stage, 4–7
Cognitive Research Trust (CoRT) System, 99, 102–105. *See also* thinking techniques
collectors, 29
communities, learning about, 12
concrete operational thinking, 13–16, 123–124
concrete props, 11, 14
conventional (organizer) personality, 92–94
COPEC (Council on Physical Education for Children), 36
CoRT (Cognitive Research Trust) System, 99, 102–105. *See also* thinking techniques
Council on Physical Education for Children (COPEC), 36

creative reasoning, 14. *See also* formal operations
creativity, 84–87
crystal radio construction, 27
curiosity and learning, 95

Damon, William, 65
de Bono, Edward, xvi, 99
delta state of arousal, 118
disequilibration/disequilibrium, 1–2
disorganized-insecure children, 56
divorce rates, 60
Don't Give Me No Lip! experiment, 19
Doyle, Arthur Conan, 94
Duffy, Frank, 107
Dunckley, V., 114
Dylan, Bob, 21

Educational Consulting and Testing, 108
EEG (electroencephalograph) waves, 109, 111
egocentric reasoning, 65–66
Einstein, Albert, 92
electroencephalogram (EEG) waves, 109, 111
Electronic Screen Syndrome, 113
emotional attachments, xiii–xiv, xvi, 5, 55, 56
emotional component to teaching, 15
emotional encouragement, 59
empathy, 43, 87–89
engagement with students, 12
enterprising (persuader) personality, 89–92
Erikson, Erik, xvi, 88. *See also* psychosocial theory
existential intelligence, 24
Experience Corps volunteers, 62
exploration, 57
eye-hand coordination of infants, 6

fairness. *See* moral development
family meetings, 70
fantasy, 8–9
fear of failure, 108
flow, 112–113
formal operations: about, 14, 16–17, 33; examples of thinking, 17–19; moral stages and, 74; stimulating, 20–21
free play, 58

Freud, Sigmund, 53
frontal lobe, 99

games, 12, 13
gamma state of arousal, 117
Gardner, Howard, x, xv, 23. *See also* multiple intelligences
Gates, Bill, 80, 89
Gem Plan for Life (Wooden), 90
generativity vs. self-absorption stage, 61
A Guide to How Children Learn (Sortino), x, xiii

hand-mouth coordination of infants, 6
Hardy, G. H., 28
Harvard's Center for Moral Development, xvii
heart's role in intelligence, 9
Heinz dilemma, 77, 122
Help Me Be Good series (Berry), 68
Hersh, R. H., 63
hippocampus, xv, xvi, 54, 79, 82, 84, 95, 99. *See also* emotional attachments
Holland, John, xvi, 80. *See also* vocational development theory
Huitt, W., 2–3, 7–8, 20–21
Hummel, J., 2–3

IB (International Baccalaureate), 29
identity vs. role confusion stage, 59–60
imagination, 8–9
incarceration, 60, 83
industry vs. inferiority stage, ix, 58–59, 85, 88
infants' views of themselves, 5, 6
initiative vs. guilt stage, 57–58, 89
instinct and behavior, 5
integrity vs. despair stage, 61–62
intelligence quotient, 23
internal combinations, understanding of, 7
International Baccalaureate (IB), 29
interpersonal conformity stage, 69–72
interpersonal intelligence, 38, 42–45
intimacy vs. isolation stage, 60–61
intrapersonal intelligence, 38, 45–48
intuition, 8, 47
investigative (thinking) personality, 94–97

juvenile offenders, 60, 83

Kamiya, Joe, 107
kindergarten classrooms, 9
kinesthetic intelligence, 35–38, 46, 48, 81–82, 84
Kohlberg, Lawrence, xvii, 122. *See also* moral development

leadership, natural, 89, 91
learning, pyramid of, 27, 122–123
learning and emotions, 9
left brain, 41
Lickona, Thomas, 69
Lindamood, Charles, 34
Lindamood, Patricia, 34
linguistic intelligence, 25–27, 44
liquids, lessons with, 13–14
logical–mathematical intelligence, 28–31. *See also* mathematics
logical/sequential world of children, 28
logical thought processes, 13, 74
"Look Out for Yourself" stage, 68–70

Magical Child (Pearce), 7, 9
Magical Child Matures (Pearce), 7, 9
magical communication, 26
magical stage. *See* preoperational stage
magic tricks, 26, 44
Maguire, Eleanor, xv
Mahler, Margaret, 5
manipulation of objects, 11, 14
marriage, 60–61
mathematics: brains/nerds, 29–31; math facts, 40; music and, 40, 41; visual-spatial ability and, 31–32
meetings, 70, 72
mental imagery, 31
Michelangelo, 79
MIDAS (Multiple Intelligence Developmental Assessment Scales), 121
Miller, John, 26
mirror neurons, 39
missing objects, understanding of, 7
mobiles, 8
modeling of behavior, 12, 74
Montessori schools: alphabet lessons, 12; art integrated in, 85; background, 24–25, 29; kinesthetic intelligence and, 36, 82; play as "work," 58

moral development: about, xvi–xvii, 59, 65; Cluster School, 77; egocentric reasoning stage, 65–66; Heinz dilemma, 77, 122; interpersonal conformity stage, 69–72, 76; respecting rights of every person stage, 73–77; responsibility to society stage, 72–74; Richard as example of, 63–64, 76–77; stay out of trouble stage, 67–68; tit-for-tat fairness stage, 68–70

Mozart Effect, 39

Mr. Roger's Neighborhood, 12

Multiple Intelligence Developmental Assessment Scales (MIDAS), 121

multiple intelligences: assessment of, 25, 121; interpersonal intelligence, 42–45; intrapersonal intelligence, 45–48; kinesthetic intelligence, 35–38, 46; linguistic intelligence, 25–27; logical–mathematical intelligence, 28–31; musical intelligence, 39–42; naturalist intelligence, 48–51; schools integrating, 24–25; spatial intelligence, 31–34

musical intelligence, 39–42

"My Way or the Cry Way" stage, 65–66

National Association for Sports & Physical Education (NAPE), 58

National Committee of State Legislators, 85–86

National Institute of Child Health and Human Development, 31

National Prison Rape Elimination Commission, 60

naturalist intelligence, 48–51

neighborhoods, learning about, 12

neoplastic responsiveness, 92

neurofeedback: about, xvii; ADHD example, 111–112, 116, 118; author's training in, 108–109; consultations, 118; EEG's role, 109–110; effectiveness, 107–108; flexibility and, 114–115; flow example, 112–113; perceptual focusing, 115; process, 109–110, 116–118, 118; PTSD example, 115–116; stress example, 112–114; transition difficulties example, 113–114; uses of, 110–111, 118

Neurofeedback Institute, 108

Nixon administration, 75

normal-symbiotic phase, 5

object permanence, 6

old brain. *See* cerebellum

operant conditioning, 110

organization, need for, 5

Othmer, S., 118, 119

part-to-whole teaching, 12, 15

Pearce, Joseph Chilton, 7, 9

peer groups, 70, 71–72

Pendulum Problem, 17

perceptual focusing, 115

performance enhancement, 112–113

Peterson, Steven E., 92

physical education, 36, 58

physical movement. *See* kinesthetic intelligence

Piaget, Jean, xv, 1–2. *See also* cognitive development stages

Piaget's Theory of Cognitive and Affective Development (Wadsworth), 1

play as "work," 58

plus, minus, interesting (PMI) approach, 100–105

Post-Traumatic Stress Disorder (PTSD), 115–116

predictability, need for, 5

prefrontal cortex, 96, 117

pregnant teens example, 63–64

preoperational stage, 8–12

primacy-recency effect, xv

Pritchard Paolitto, D., 63

problem-solving skills, 16. *See also* formal operations; investigative (thinking) personality

The Promised Cookie (Sortino), x

psychosexual theory, 53

psychosocial theory: about, xvi; autonomy vs. doubt and shame stage, 55–56; generativity vs. self-absorption stage, 61; identity vs. role confusion stage, 59–60; industry vs. inferiority stage, 58–59; initiative vs. guilt stage, 57–58; integrity vs. despair stage, 61–62; trust vs. mistrust stage, 53–55

PTSD (Post-Traumatic Stress Disorder), 115–116
punishment-focused thinking, 67–68
pyramid of learning, 27, 122–123

reactive attachment disorder (RAD), 5, 55, 108, 118
reading process/skills: brain structure and, 10; detective stories, 95; fairy tales, 92; music influencing, 40; spatial ability influencing, 31, 33
realistic, investigative, artistic, social, enterprising, and conventional (RIASEC) career themes, xvi. *See also* careers matched to multiple intelligences; vocational development theory
realistic personality, 81–84
real-world connections, 25
Reimer, J., 63
"Reinventing the Wheel" (National Committee of State Legislators), 85–86
relationships, 70
Reset Your Child's Brain (Dunckley), 114
resistant-insecure children, 56
respect for every person stage, 73–77
responsibility to society stage, 72–74
RIASEC (realistic, investigative, artistic, social, enterprising, and conventional), xvi. *See also* vocational development theory
Richard (moral development example), 63–64, 76–77
right brain, 41
Robbins, J., 118
role confusion, 60

schemas, 4
school programs. *See* Montessori schools; Waldorf schools
Schraf, P., 122
scientific experiments, 15
securely attached children, 56
SED (seriously emotionally disturbed) program, 63
self-regulation of behavior, 56–57, 110, 114
Selman, Robert, 65
sensory and motor exploration, 4–8

separation-individuation theory of child development, 5
sequential reinforcement, 32
sequential world of children, 28
seriously emotionally disturbed (SED) program, 63
sharing of experiences, 12, 89–90
Sharon's dilemma, 72–73
Sirkin, A., 27
skill learning model, 110
social (helper) personality, 87–89
social interaction, 8
social issue discussions, 20–21
social media, 91
Sousa, David, x, 3, 10
spatial intelligence, 31–34, 84
spectacle method, 102
Spielberg, Steven, 80
spoken language. *See* linguistic intelligence
sports, 36–38
sportsmanship, 90
Steinber, M., 118
Steiner, Rudolf, xv, 29
step-by-step explanations, 20
Sterman, Barry, 107
story characters, 16
story diagrams, 20
story maps, 33
story problems, 16
"Strange Situation" experiences, 55–56
stress, 96, 112–114
Suzuki method, 41
A Symphony in the Brain (Robbins), 118
synaptogenesis, 85

tactile learners. *See* kinesthetic intelligence
theater groups, 44
theta state of arousal, 117
thinking techniques, xvi, 99–105
timing of classroom lessons, xv
"Tit-for-Tat Fairness" stage, 68–70
toys, 8
trust vs. mistrust stage, 53–55
Two Girls at a Dance experiment, 18–19

University of California, 40

violence, 8

violin playing, 41
visual aids, 20
vocational development theory. *See also* careers matched to personality types: about, xvi, 79–80; artistic personality, 84–87; assessments, 80; conventional (organizer) personality, 92–94; enterprising (persuader) personality, 89–92; investigative (thinking) personality, 94–97; realistic personality, 81–84; social (helper) personality, 87–89
volunteer activities, 62, 70, 86, 87

Wadsworth, Barry, 1
Waldorf schools, 12, 24, 85
Watergate hearings, 75
"What Will Others Think of Me?" stage, 69–72
"Who Am I" question, 60
whole-to-part teaching, 12, 16, 32–33
why questions, 25, 29
win at all costs attitude, 90–91
Wooden, John, 90
"zoo zoo" class, x

About the Author

David P. Sortino (Ed.M., Ph.D.) holds a master's degree in human development from Harvard University and a doctorate in clinical psychology from Saybrook University, as well as learning handicapped, resource specialist, and multiple subject teaching credentials. Over the last forty years, he has served as a director to several residential school programs of LH and SED students in public and private education at the elementary, middle, and secondary school levels. He has served as a consultant to state and county programs for at-risk youth (juvenile hall) and special needs children and works directly with individuals and families.

In his private practice, Sortino consults and collaborates with students, parents, teachers, and psychologists to provide support for students in pre-K through college in establishing school success and higher learning levels. He finds that exploring how the brain learns, as well as other learning strategies, can help students develop a better understanding of learning in and out of the classroom. Currently, he directs the Neurofeedback Institute, writes a blog for the *Santa Rosa Press Democrat*, and hosts a bimonthly radio show called *Brain Smart: A Better Learning Brain* on KOWS, 98.7 FM. He is the author of *The Promised Cookie: No Longer Angry Children* (2011) and *A Guide to How Your Child Learns: Understanding the Brain from Infancy to Young Adulthood* (2017).